TRAVIS 'RMNS13' BRADLEY'S

WASHINGTON
Inktober 2014 + Other Visual Rations

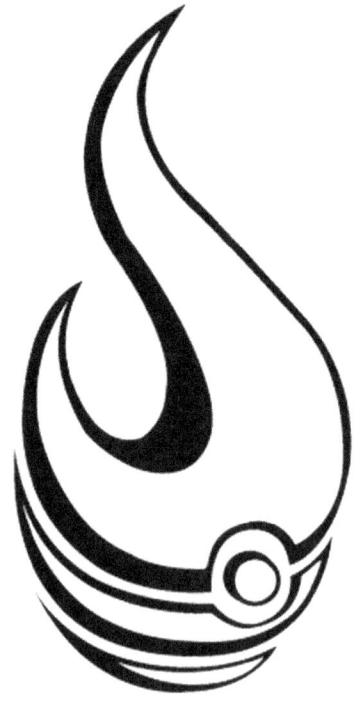

Art & Layout by Travis Bradley

This book is dedicated to my late grandfather,

CHARLES R. BRADLEY

07/22/1922 - 06/28/2004

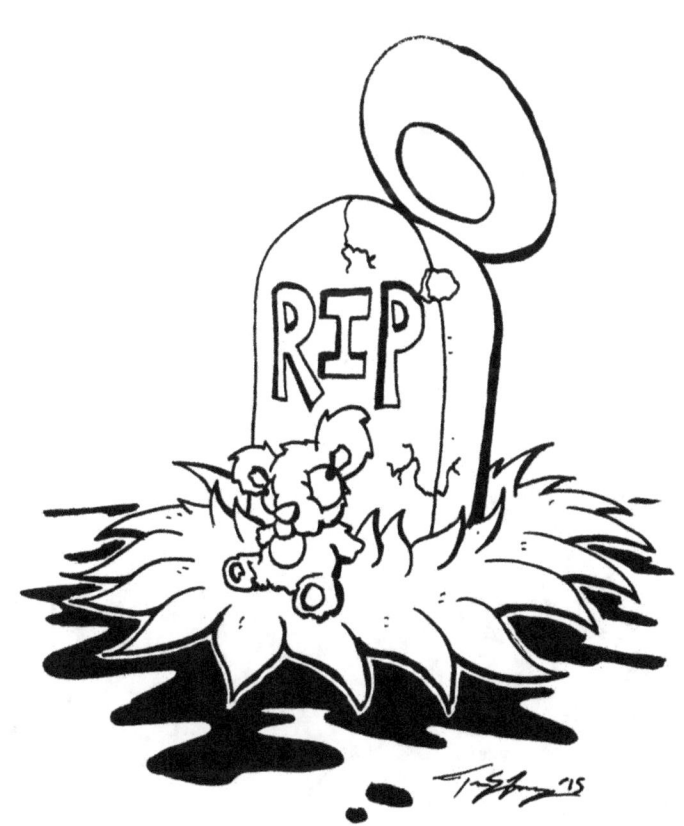

[A FORWARD THAT'S NOT TOO] [FORWARD]

Well, I was asked by a dear friend of mine to write a little blurb about how we met, and what it was like being his friend all these years for a book he was making. My first reaction was "wait, he's an Artist not a Writer, there is no way this is real". After talking to him a bit longer it appears that he was telling the truth...

Where do I even begin with the adventures we have had over the years? It all started in 5th grade at Stevens Elementary- Travis ran up to me, no introduction, no names, just a roar. At first I was a little thrown back at what had just happen, but then I realized he just really liked Jurassic Park. High School is really when our friendship took off, thanks to Mr. Semon's History classes. Those classes were the highlight of my High School career, and having Travis as a classmate made it all the better. The adventures we have been through- from the trip to Rotterdam Square Mall where we pretended to be Refrigerator Salesmen at Sears all the way to the 3 hour road trip we took to Boston this year to see a public showing of "Digging Up The Marrow" in the dead of winter. It's all been a blast.

Having Travis in my life has really been something that I could not live without. Between the wits that he brings to the table all the way to his laugh that you can't help but laugh at. We have made many memories, and have had a lot of laughs. I've Learned a lot from Travis, and I hope that he is around to influence the kids that I will probably never have.

As the artist Sheppard so wisely put it as we drove around for an hour trying to find that Boston Theater...

"SAY GERONIMO!"

-Alex Braman

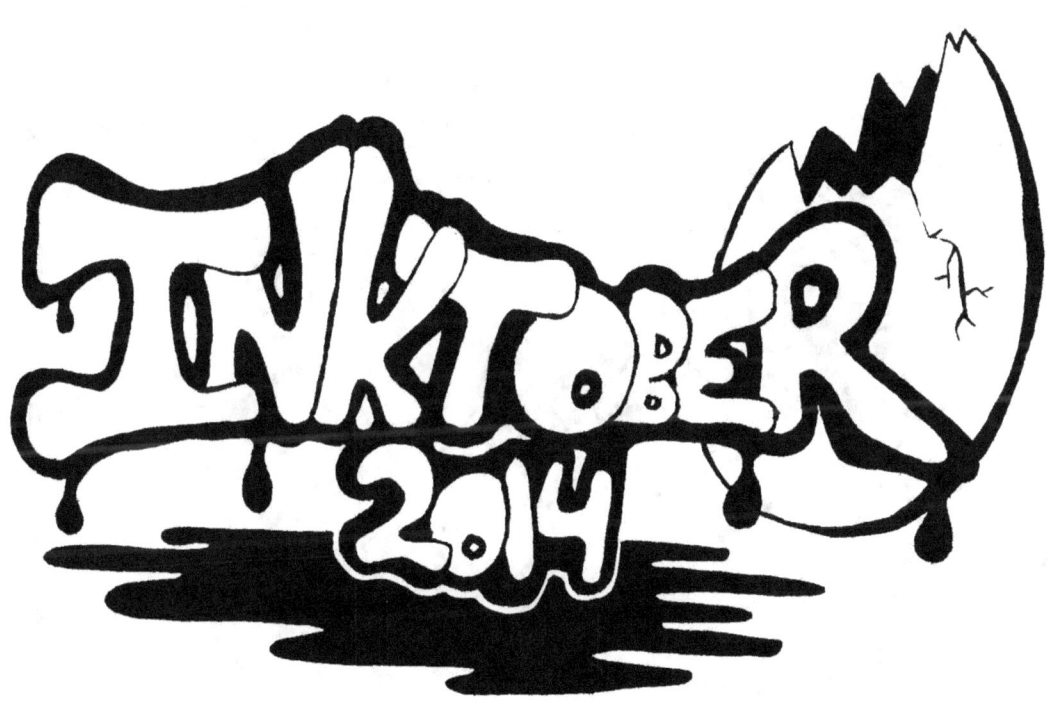

all work dates between October 1st-November 6th, 2014

Spidermander

DAY 1

The Terror of Big Ben

DAY 2

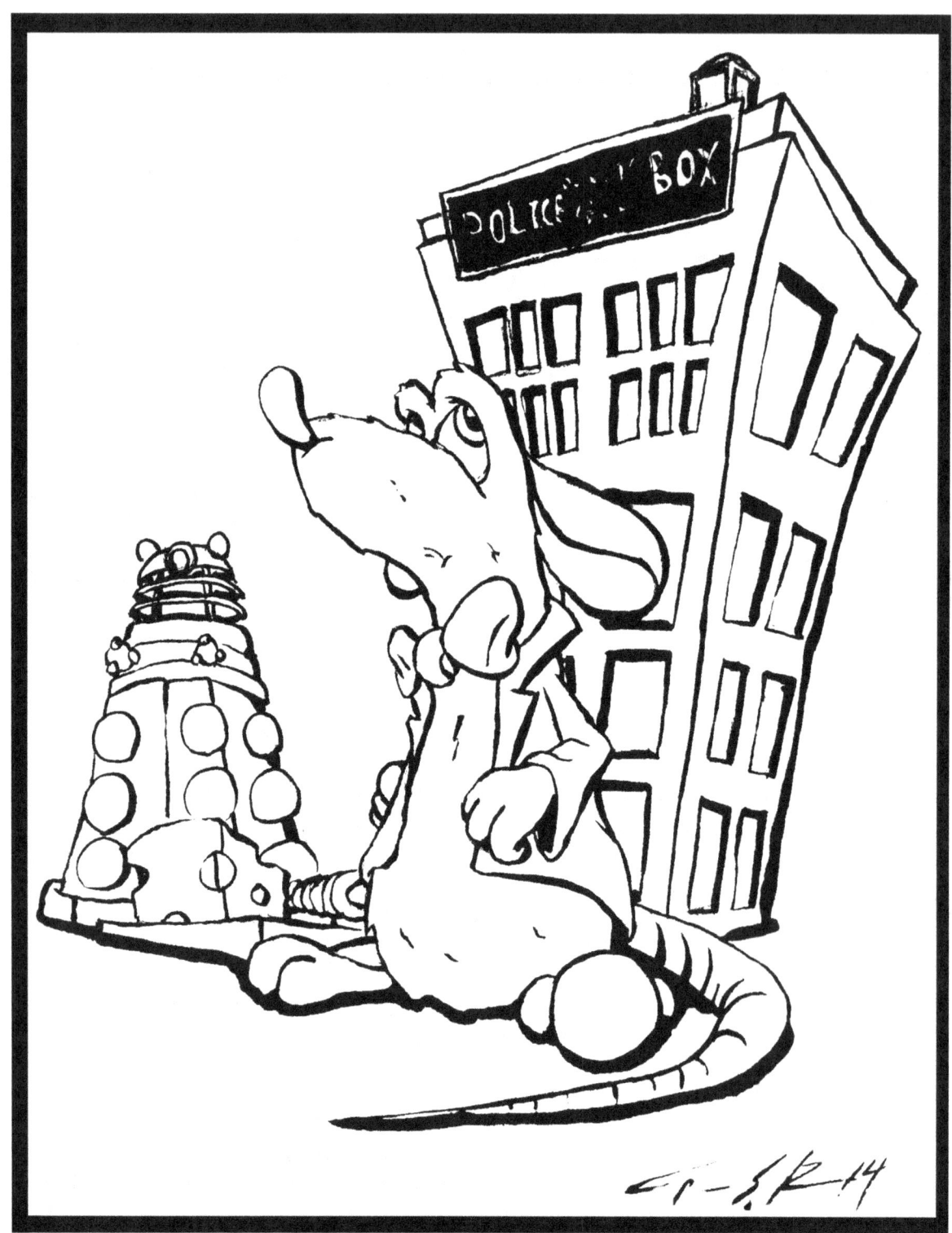

Ratawhoee

DAY 3

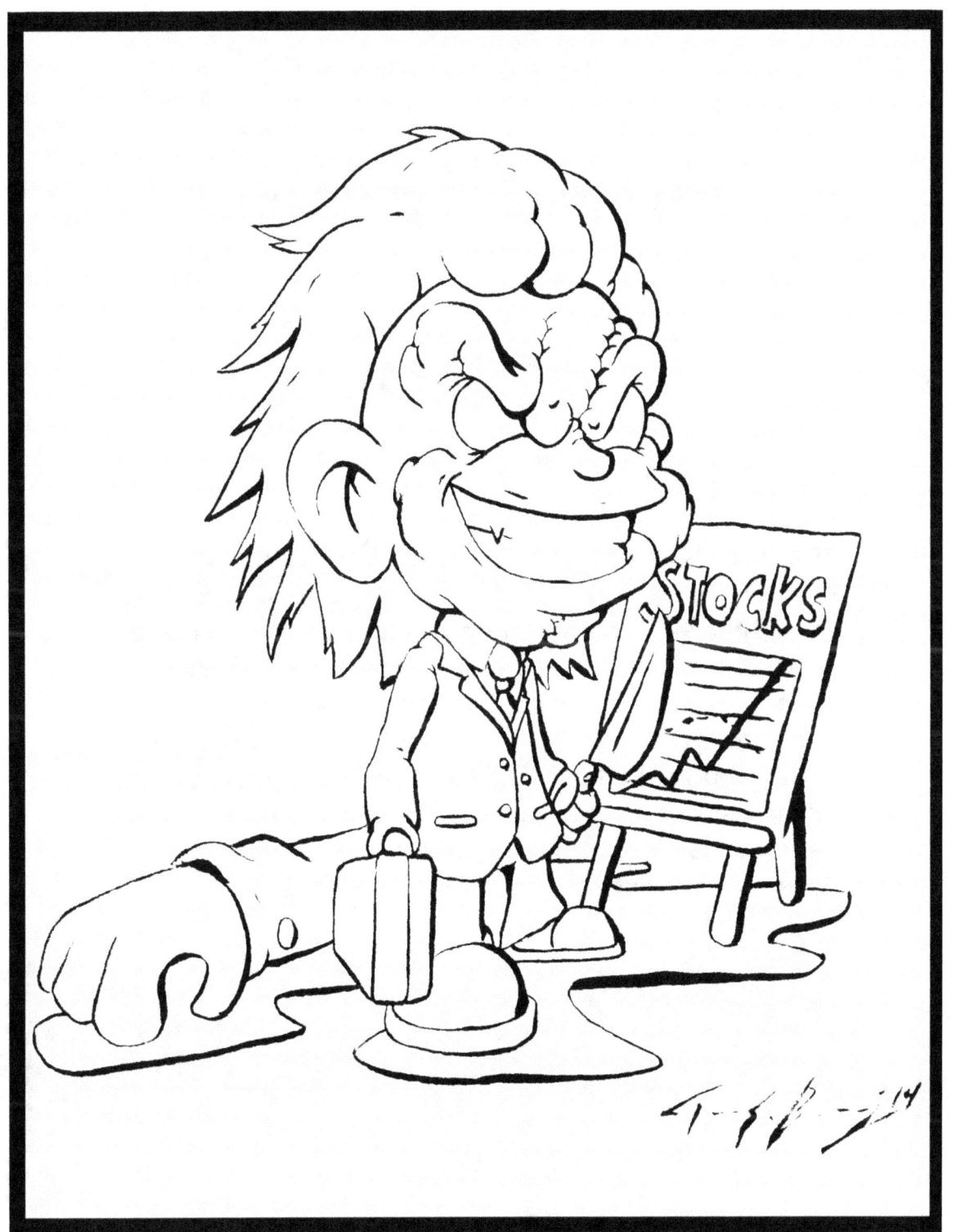

Victory Chuckle

DAY 4

The Most Evil Hare

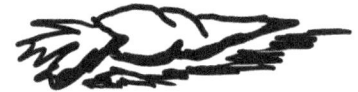

Fillister was once the trusted Guardian of the Crown Jewel Ring. That was until his deception in 1804. Swayed by the evil Hare Nibble whose ultimate pursuit was to enslave England with the ancient power of the Crown Jewels, enabling his taking of every piece of Karot gold the land had to offer. We know today that plot never came to be, but that doesn't mean society isn't still paying the price of Nibble's dark conquest...

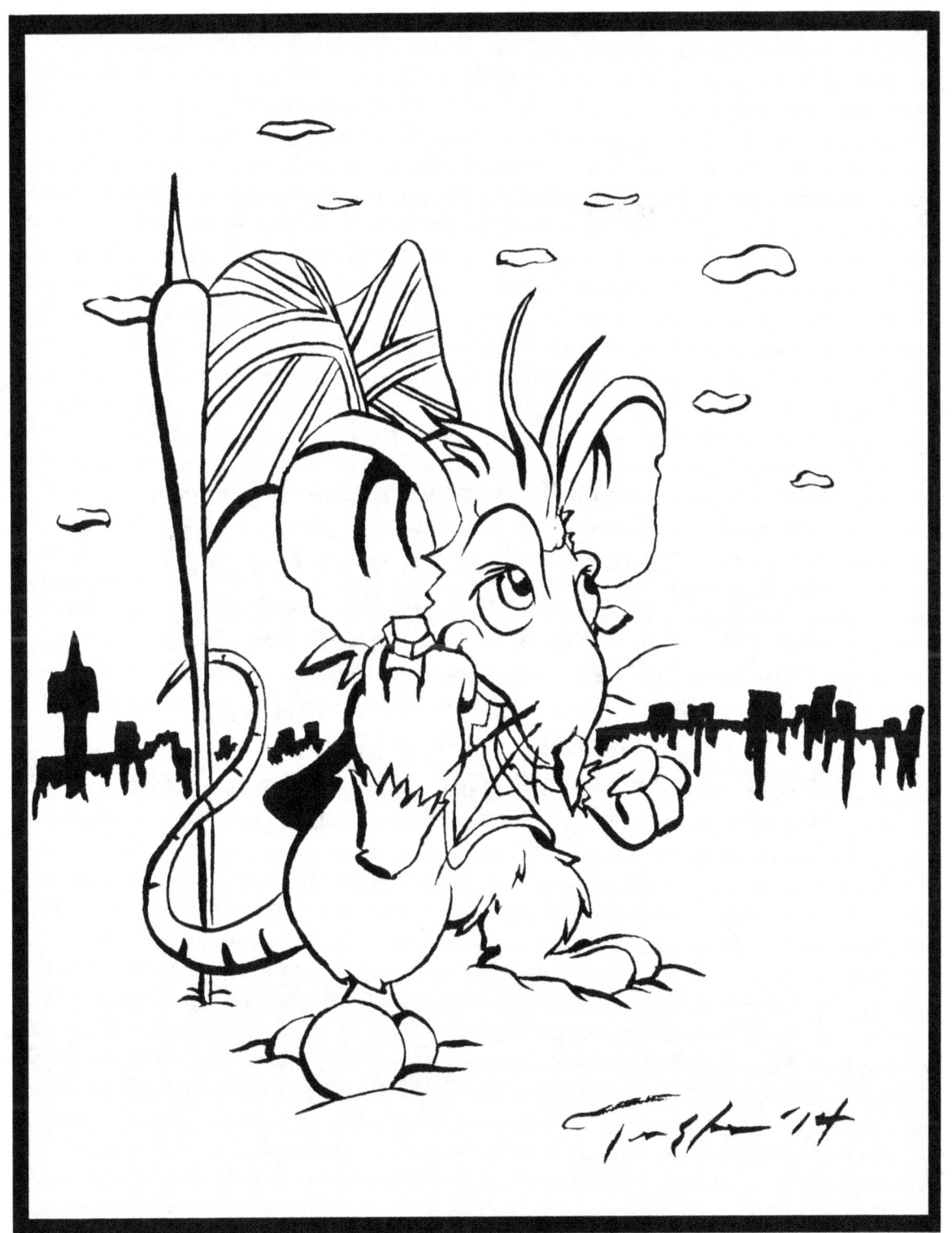

Fillister (Guardian of the Ring)

DAY 5

The Most Evil Hare

Fodder could tell Fillister wasn't acting normal even from the very first day NIbble deceived him. Confronting the issue was far from wise; so Fodder let him be. It wouldn't be long before Fodder would regret this. Soon after Fillisters' influence on Fodder would turn him to join Nibbles' forces. Of course this was all attributted to Nibbles' mind control; regardless the ripple effect these events would have on the lives of both mice would be eternal.

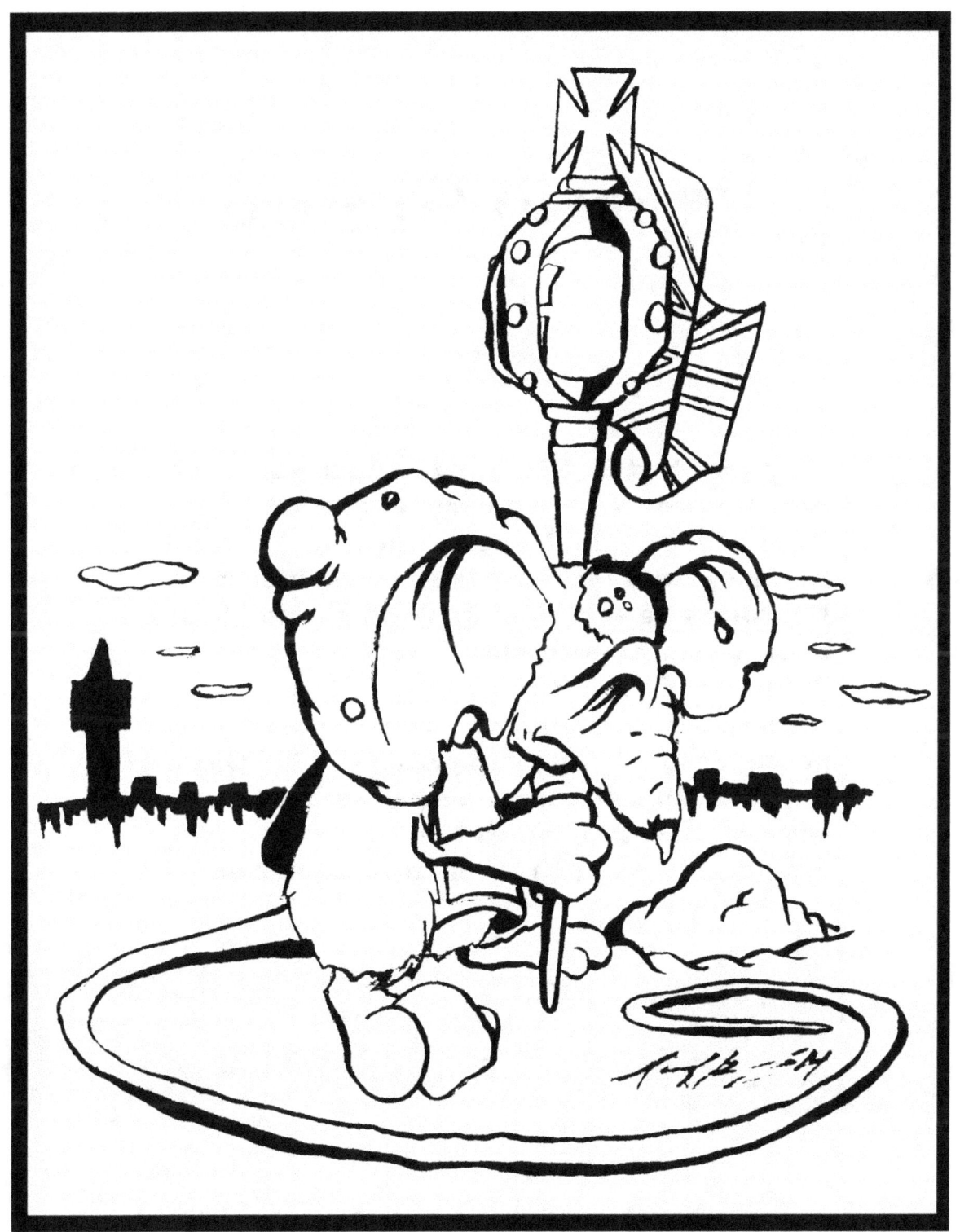

Fodder (Guardian of the Scepter)

DAY 6

The Most Evil Hare

Wayward had Fillister, and Fodder gone . The King was now aware a darkness lurked among his people. Never suspecting it would be those from his most trusted cabinet of Guardians he sent Sankin, Fodder, and Fillister to scout the countryside. The King was determined to blot out this evil that threatened to disrupt the two-hundred year peace his family line had preserved for those of England. Only Martin the King's most trusted warrior stayed to guard the King in case evil intended to meet them at their doorstep.

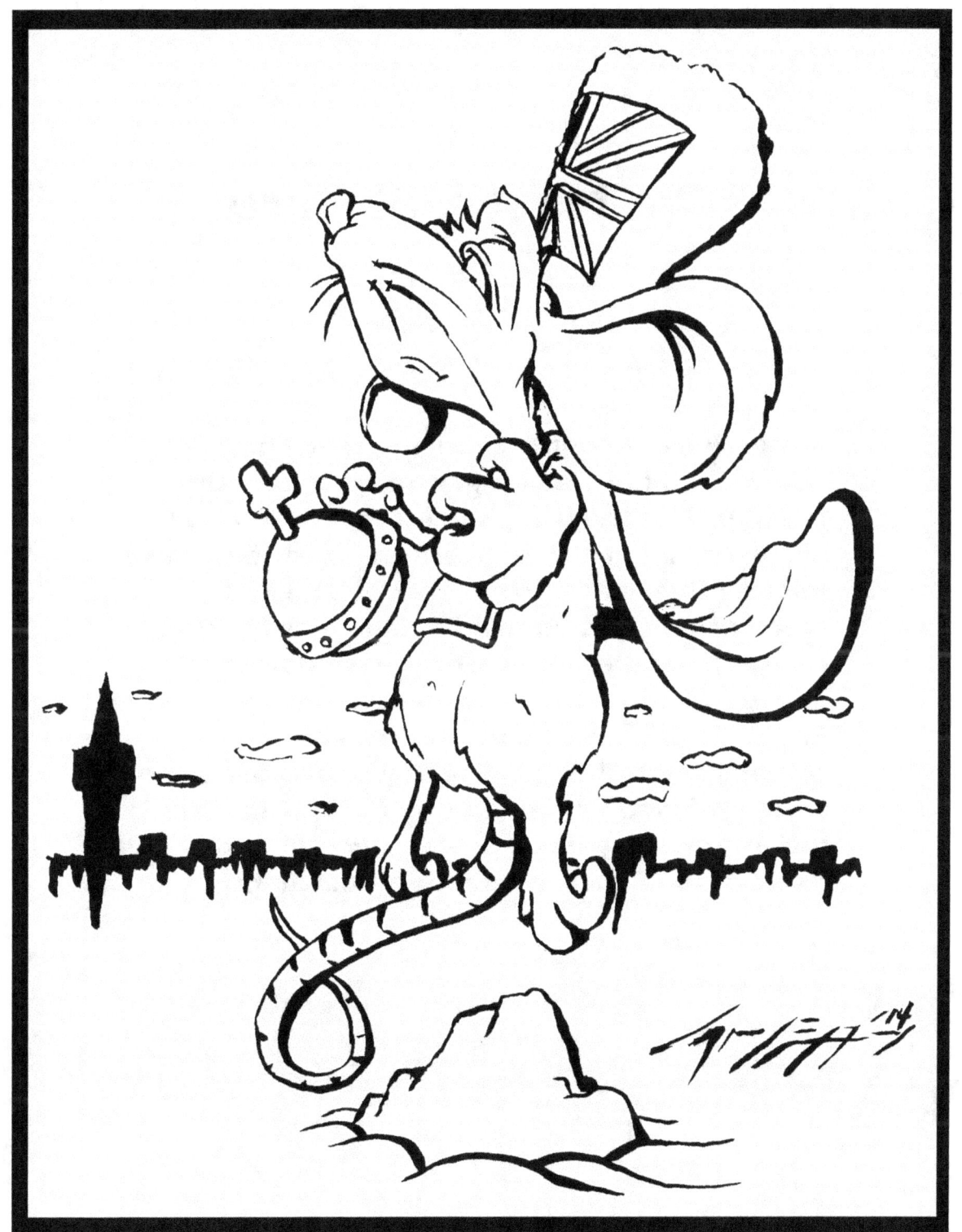

Sankin (Guardian of the Orb)

DAY 7

The Most Evil Hare

Times were certainly changing. The Guardian trio were taking far longer on their scouting mission than the King had intended. Against his instict he ordered Martin to track down the missing Guardians. Whatever evil lurked among them was an evil England was far from ready to handle. The throne wasn't safe; no one was. Unless the Guardians could be found. Englands' fate rested in the paws of a seemingly invisbile mouse now scurrying out of the city. Martin only had one option- find the missing crown jewels; preferably still in the ownership of their respective Guardians.

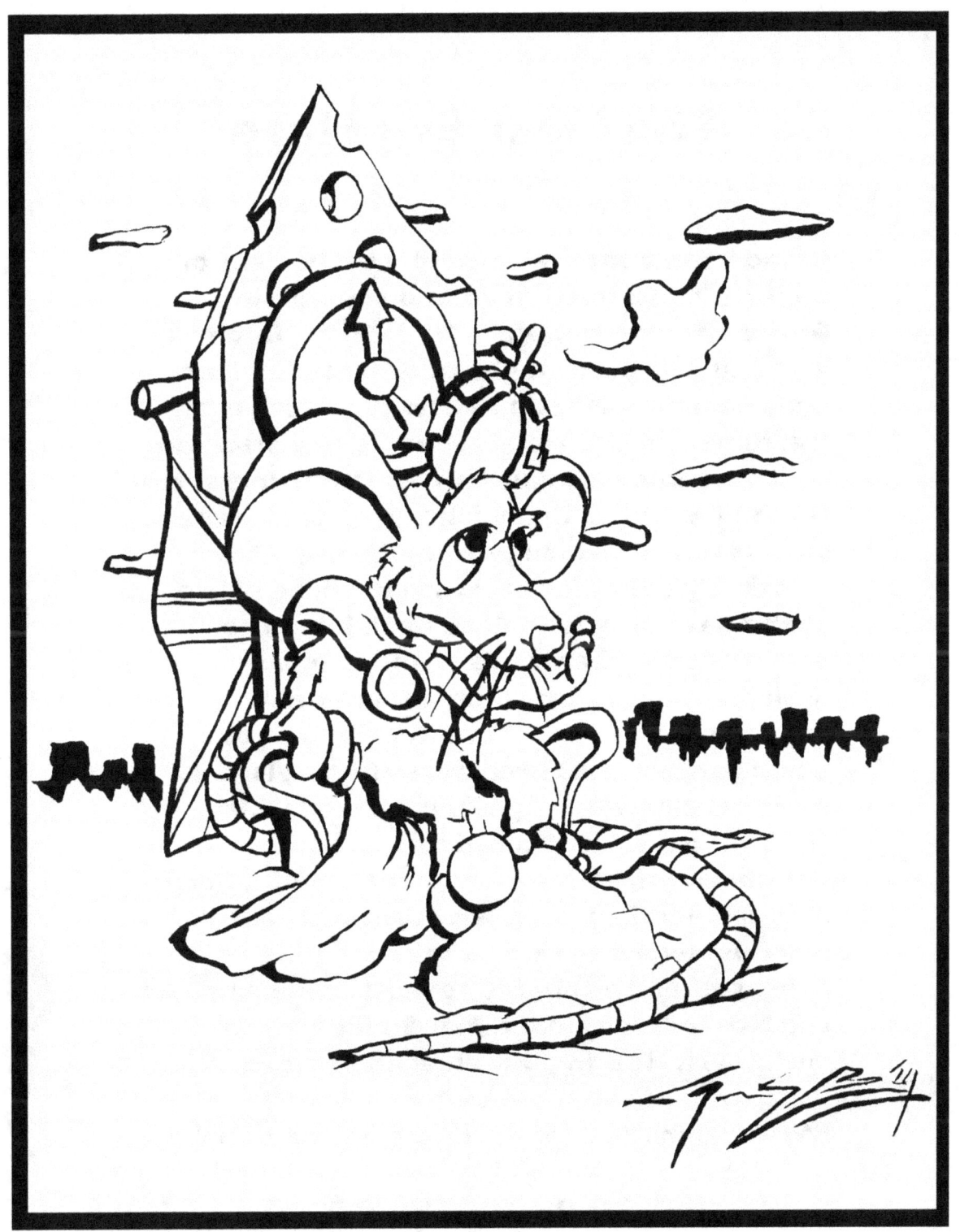

King Toil VIII (Guardian of the Throne)

DAY 8

The Most Evil Hare

It had been a month since Martin had set out on King Toils' mission to find the missing Guardians, and hopefully in doing so find the growing evil that sought to destroy England. Unfortunately Martin had no luck. Not even the fungus of the woods seemed any stronger, which we know fungus thrives in darkness! Nor could he find the Guardians. Well that was until Martins' return journey through the woods. There before him stood three figures at the base of what had to have been the oldest tree in the woods. Though Martin desired to approach them a force field generated by Sankins' orb kept him at bay. Upon contact the three mice shot a glare in Martins' direction- eyes now glazed white. Nibbles' deceit had consumed them. Channeling their life energy they shot a beam through Fodders' scepter. Almost insantly Martins' sword seemd to take on a life of its' own as it led the charge towards the beam. As the two forces collided Martin faded into darknesss. Hearing but an echo of words...

'Where light resides darkness has no home."

to be continued
(see "Adams: Inktober 2015 + Other Visual Rations")

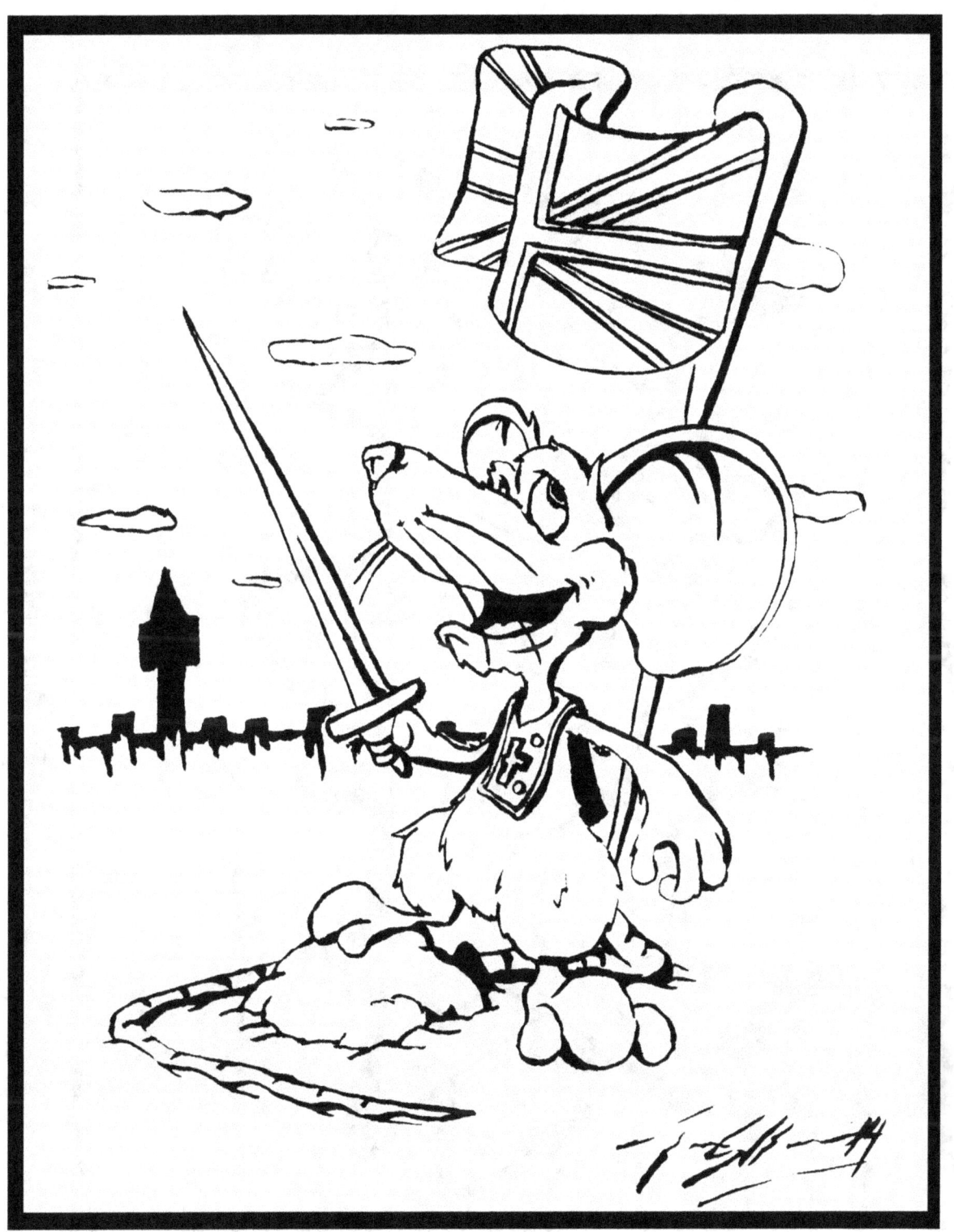

Martin (Guardian of the Sword)

DAY 9

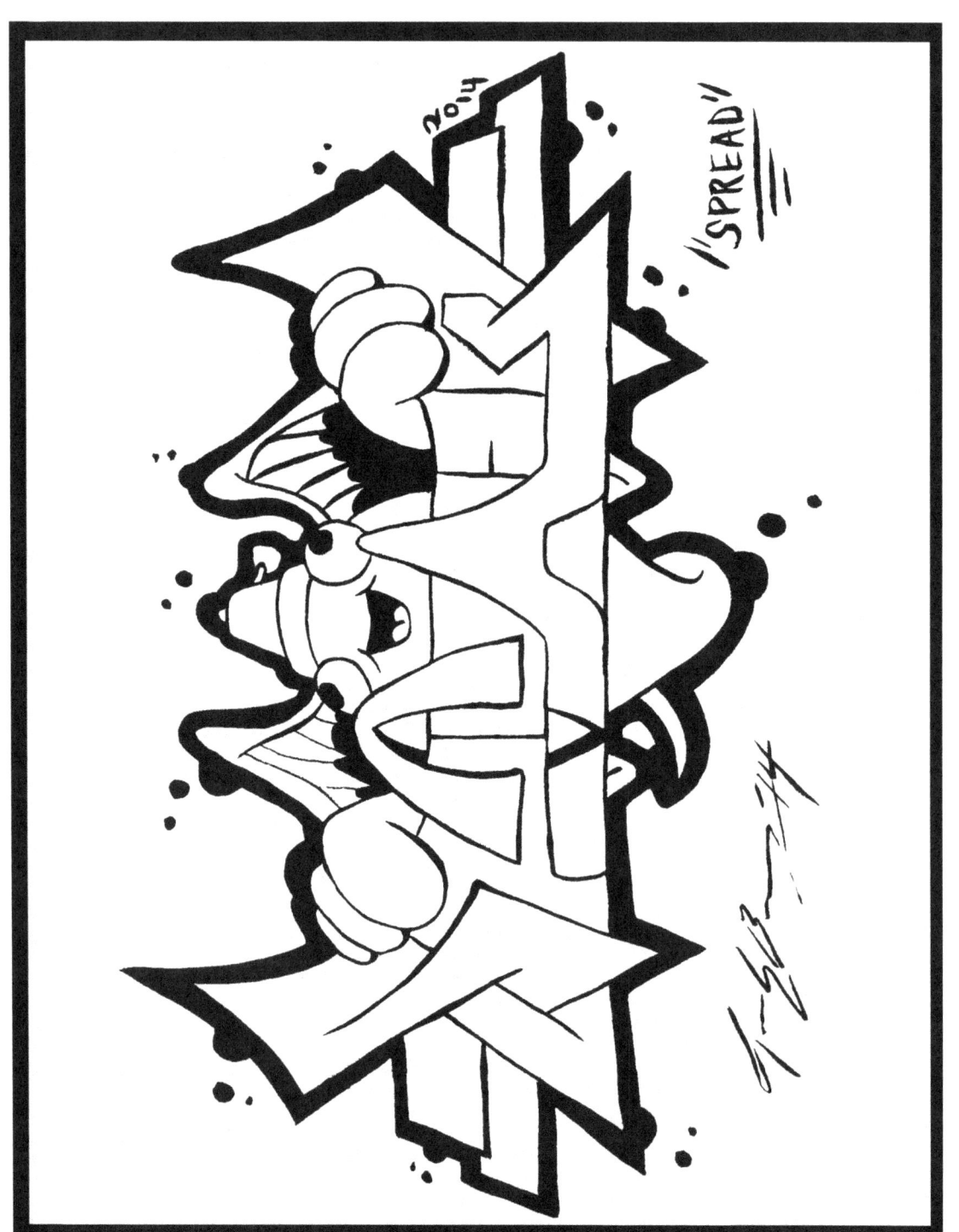

SPREAD (No. 1)

DAY 10

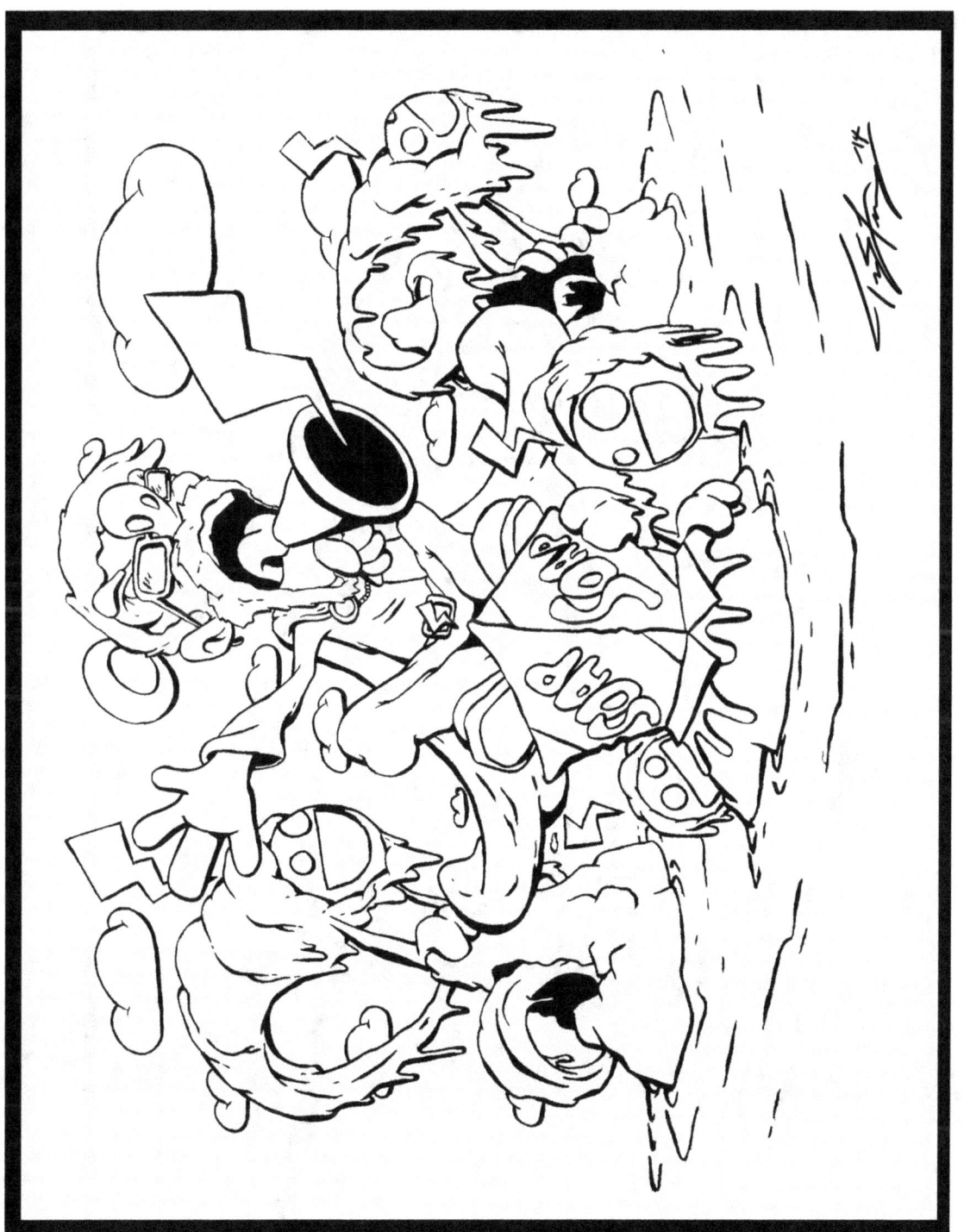

Keyte, The Banter King

DAY 11

Foreign Fast Food

DAY 12

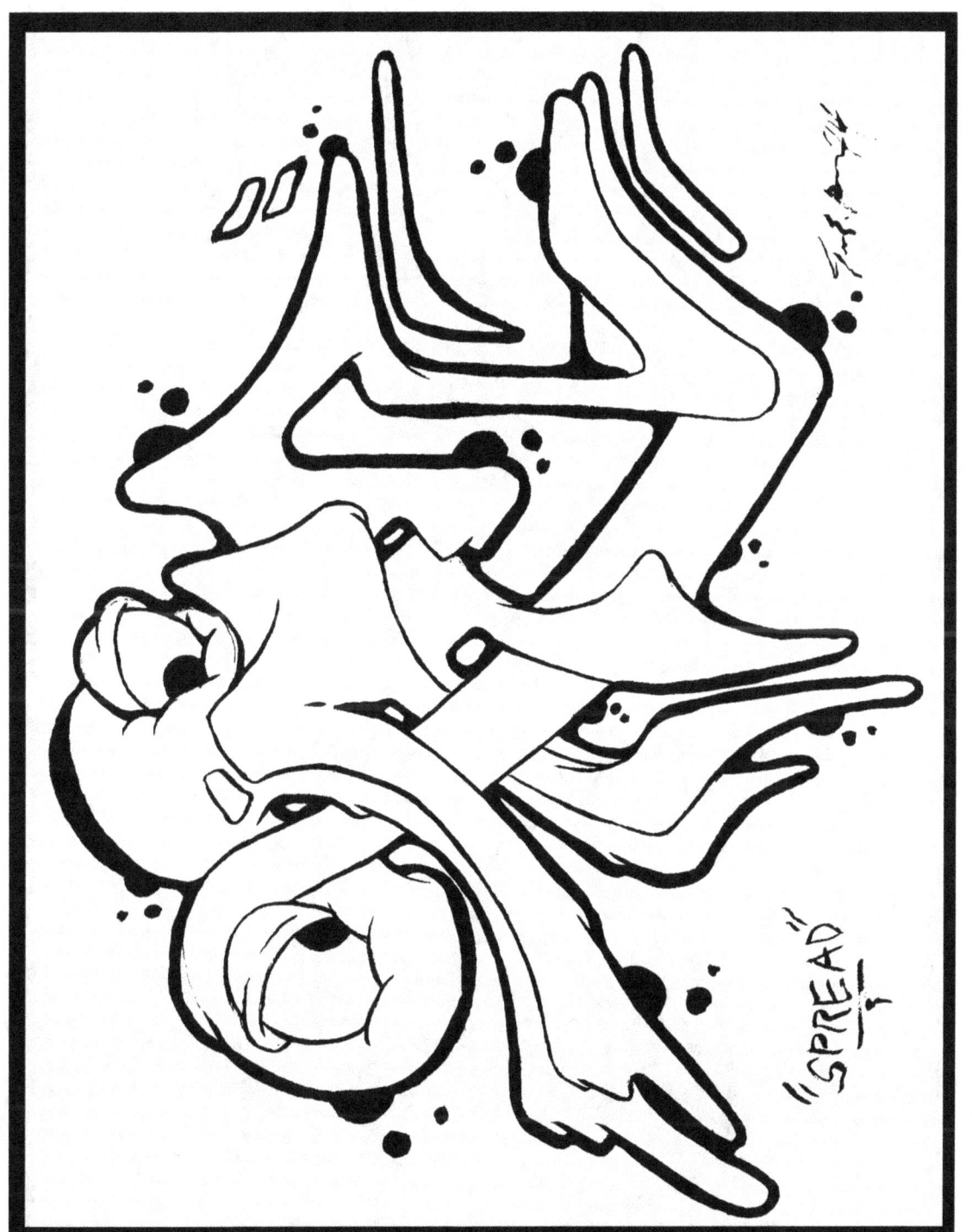

SPREAD (No.2)

DAY 13

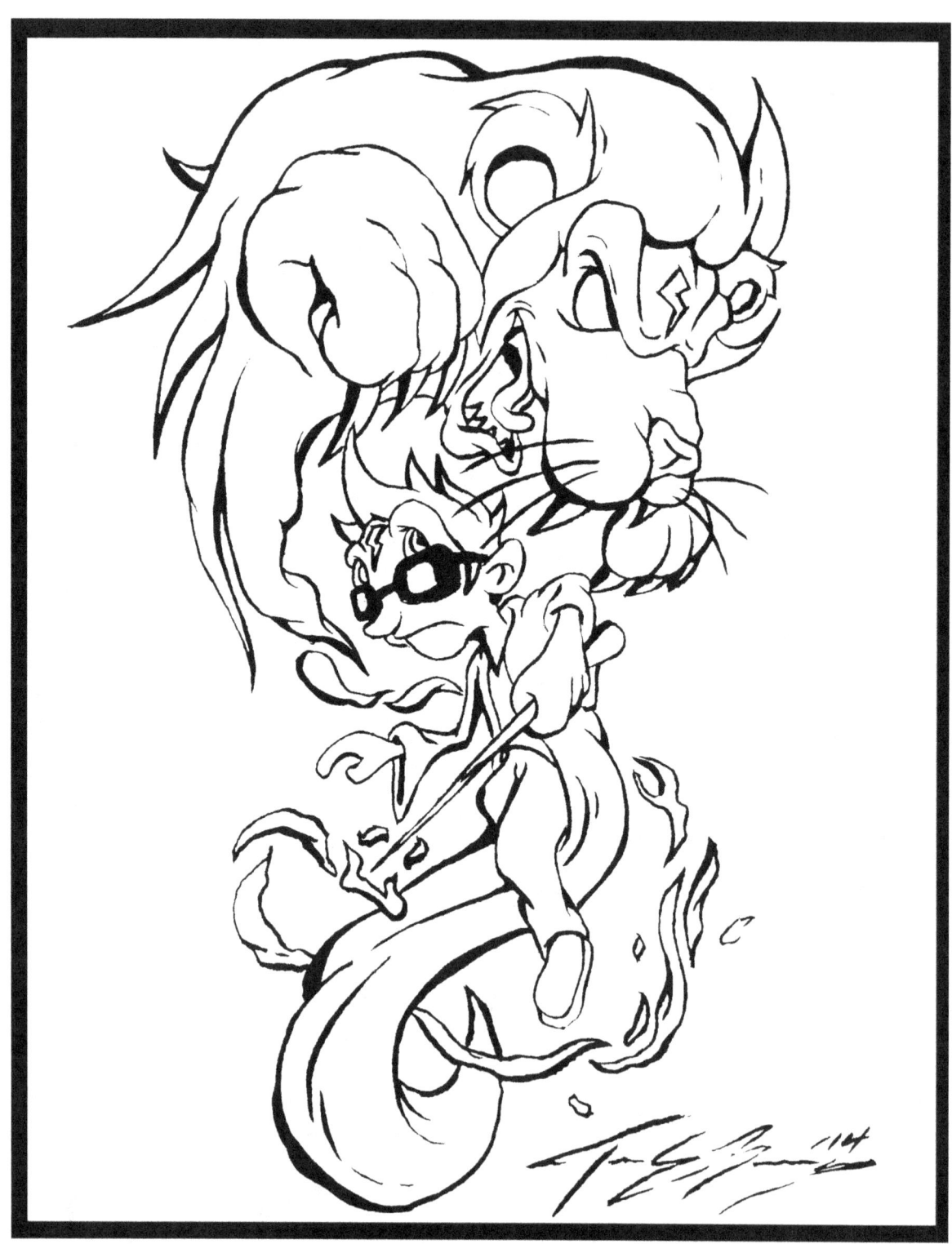

The Spirit of Gryffindor

DAY 14

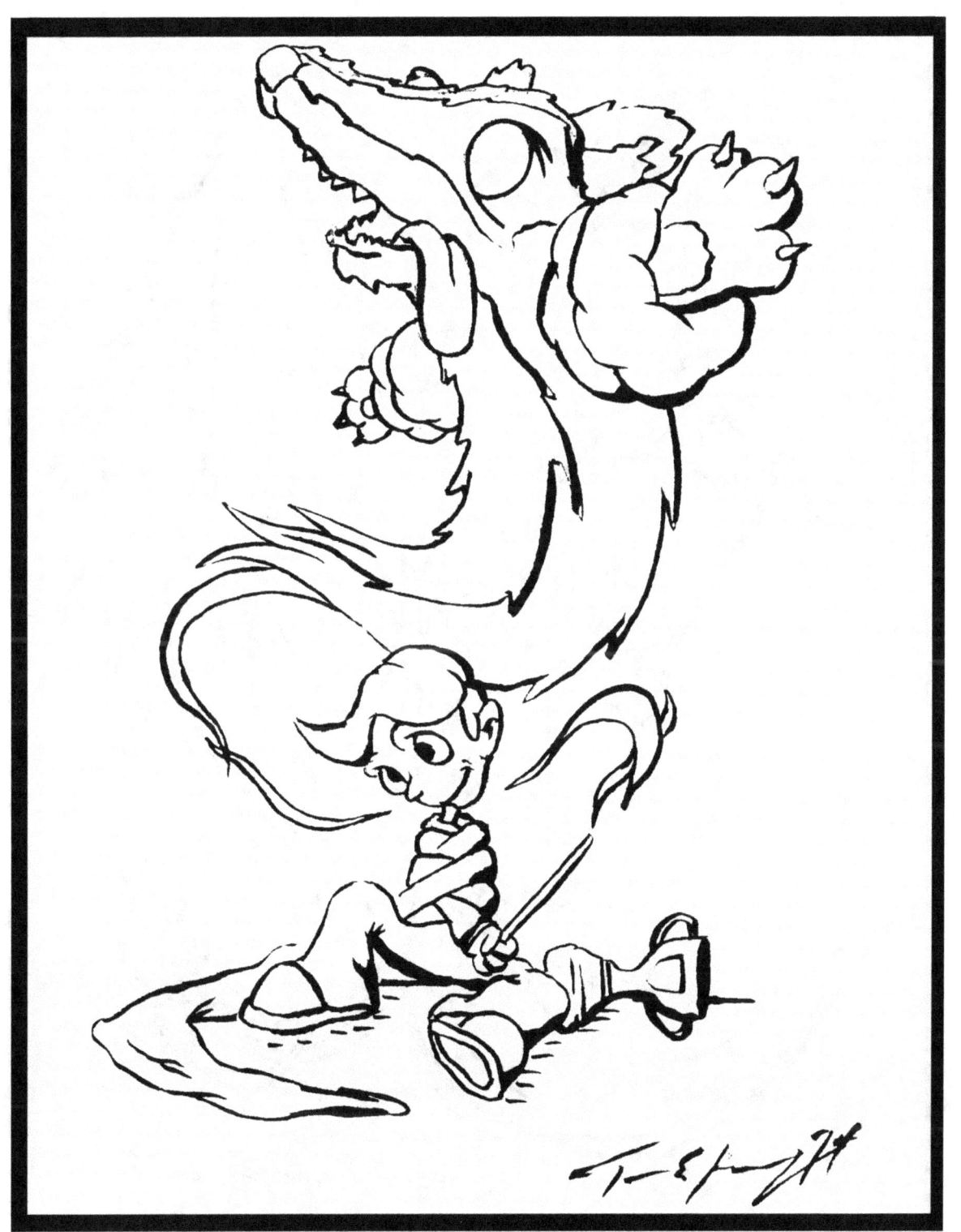

The Spirit of Hufflepuff

DAY 15

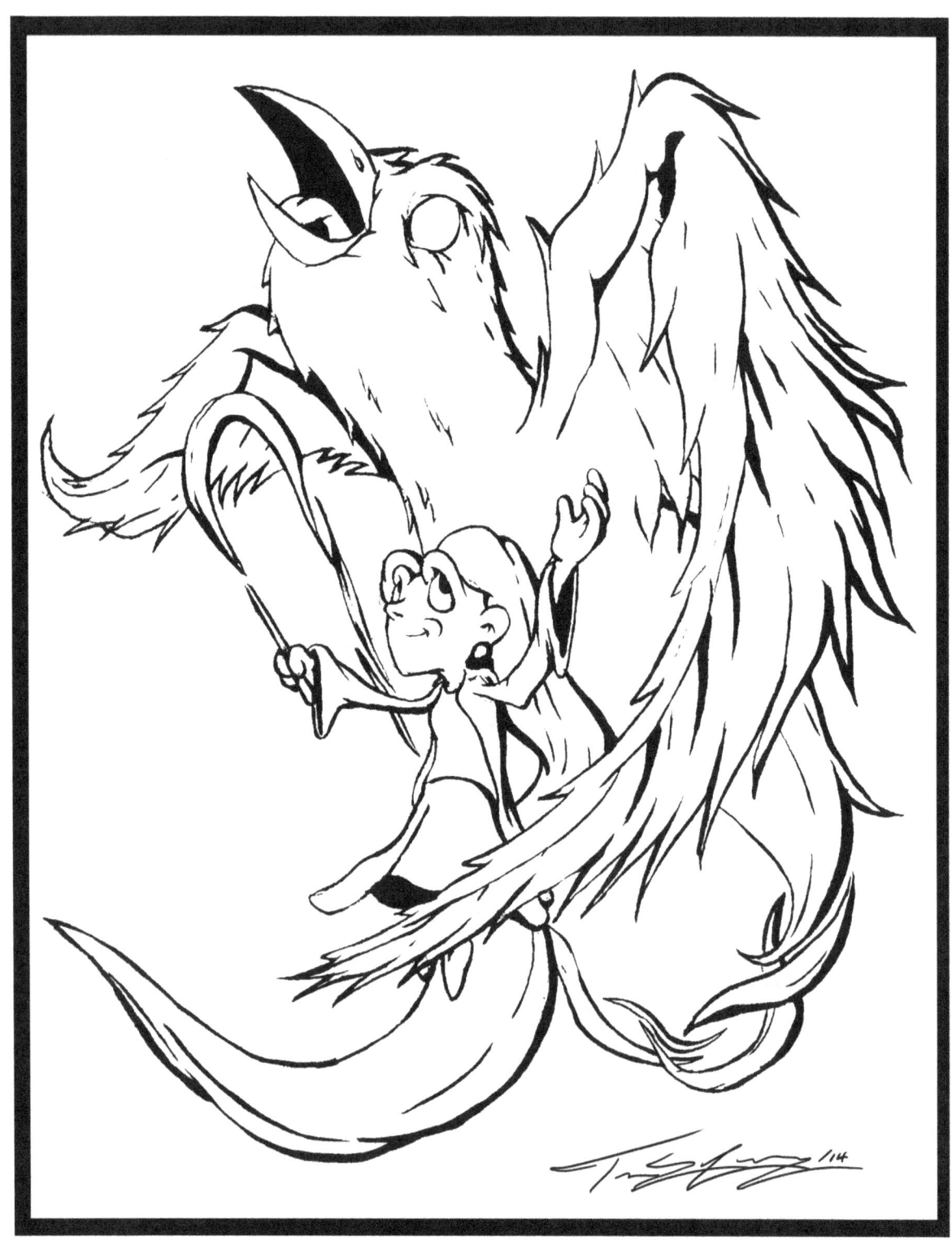

The Spirit of Ravenclaw

DAY 16

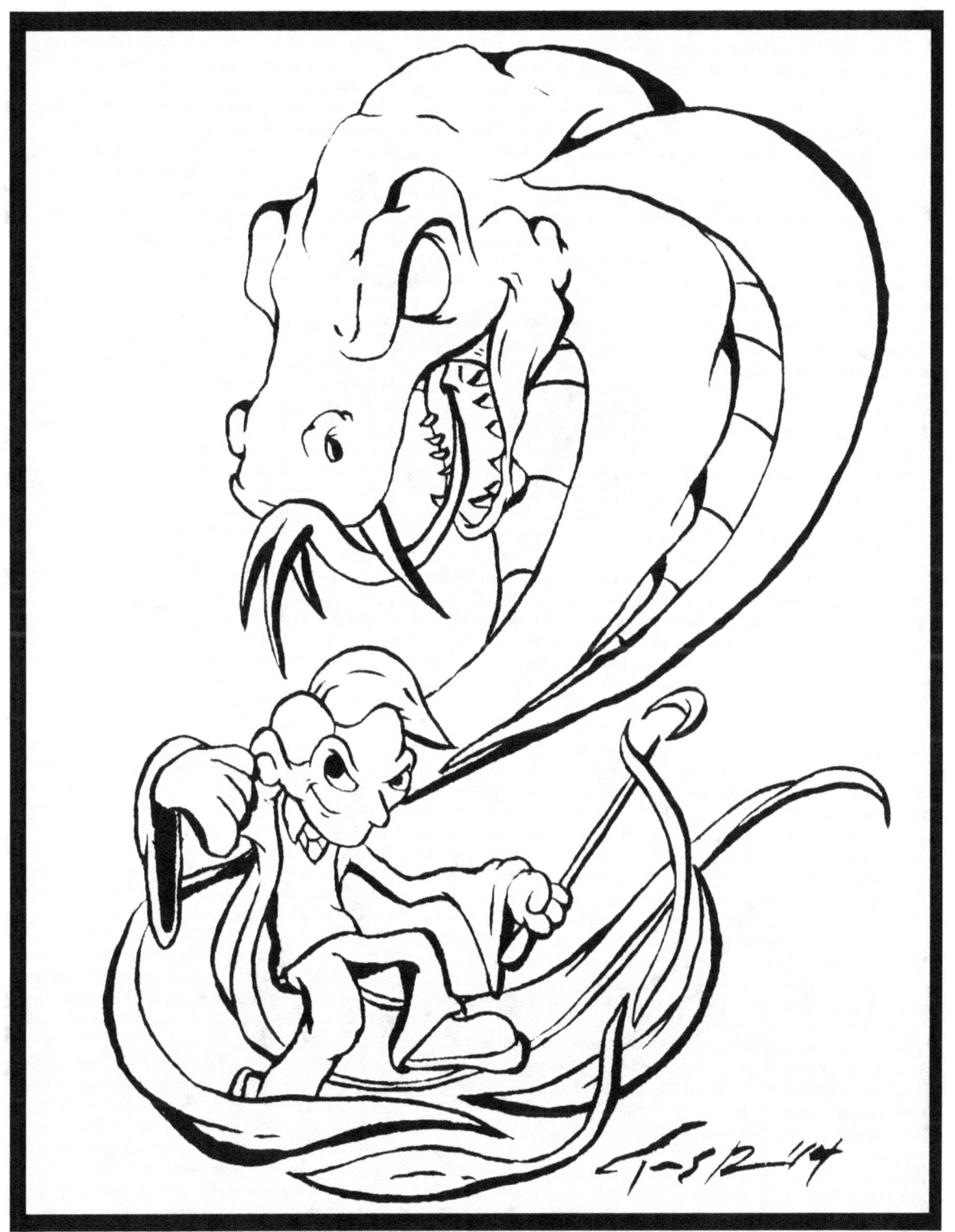

The Spirit of Slytherin

DAY 17

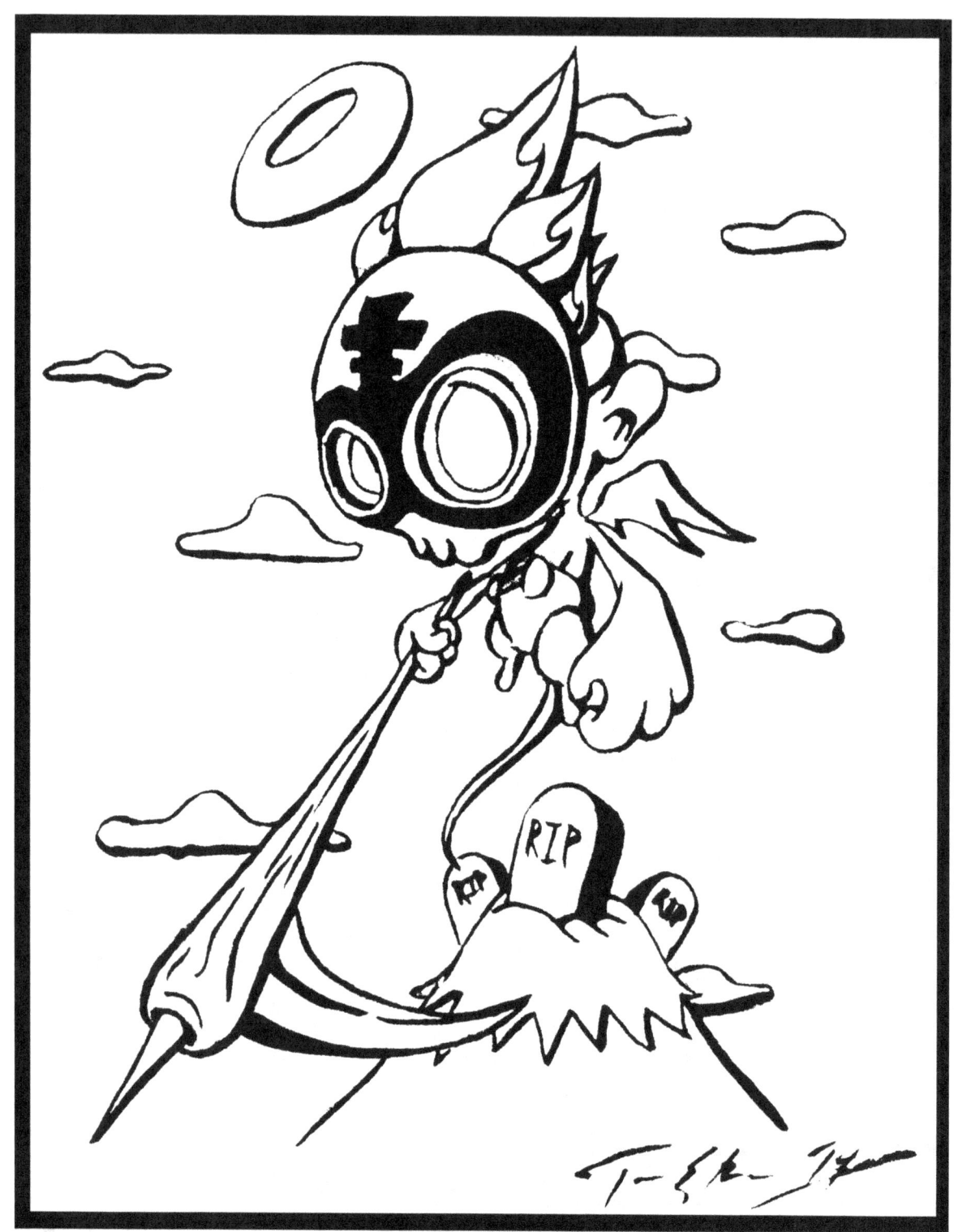

Reaper Ru

DAY 18

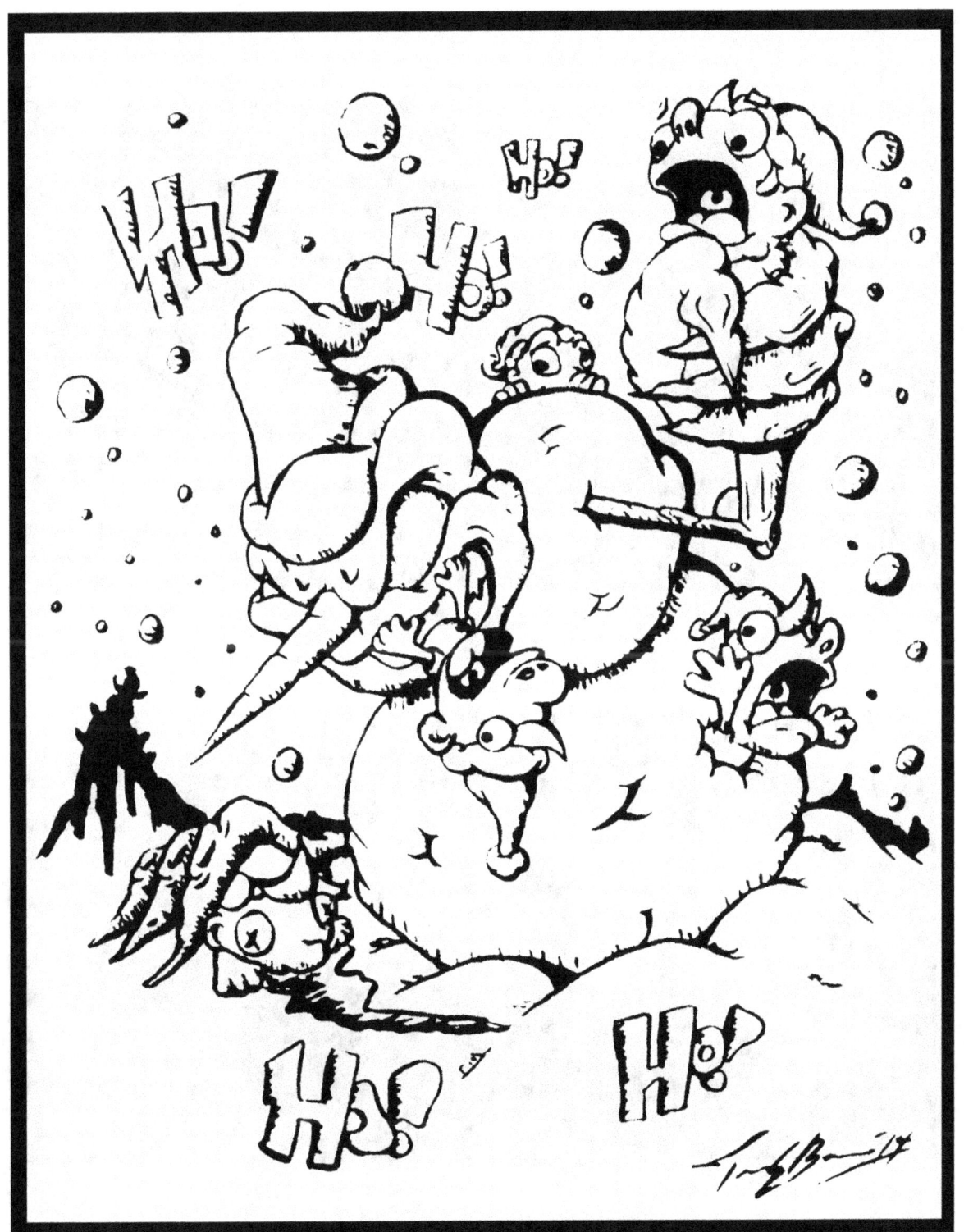

Fatal Frostbite

DAY 19

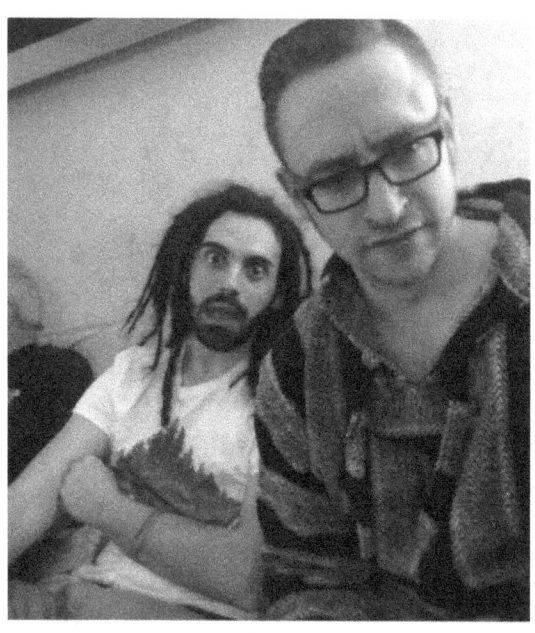
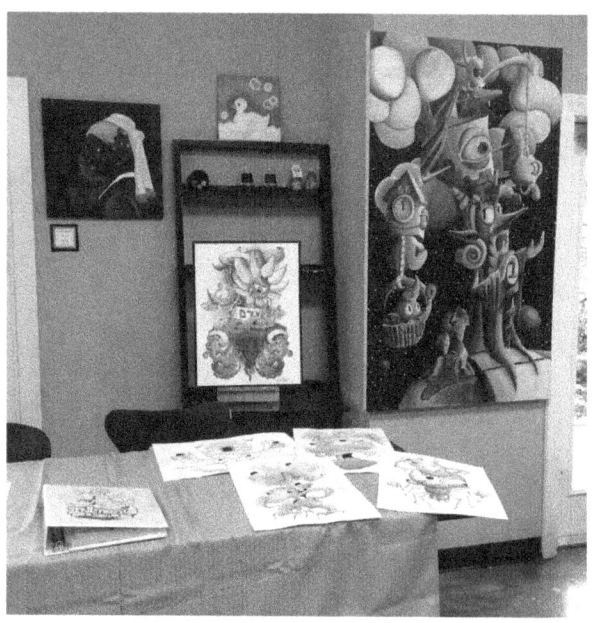
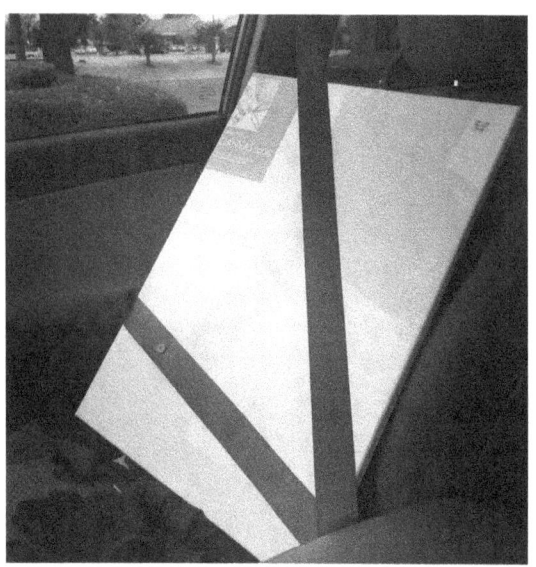
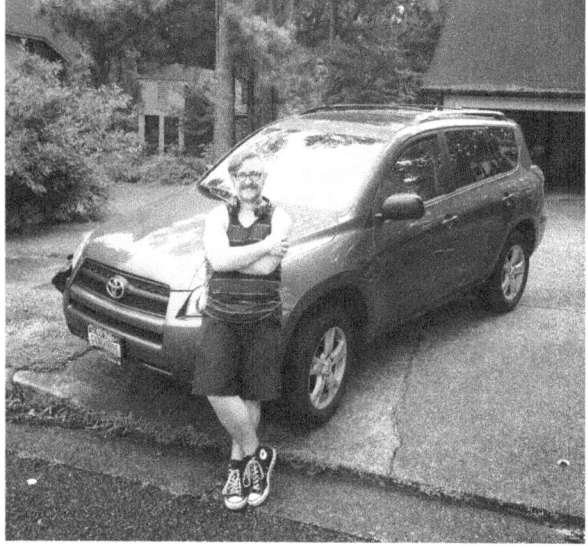

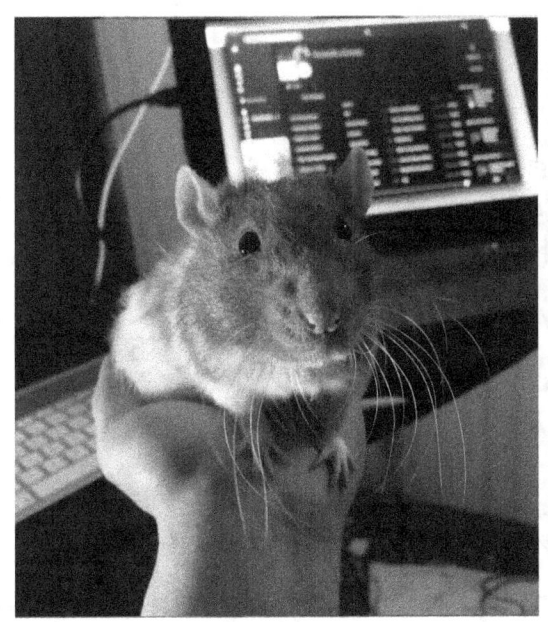
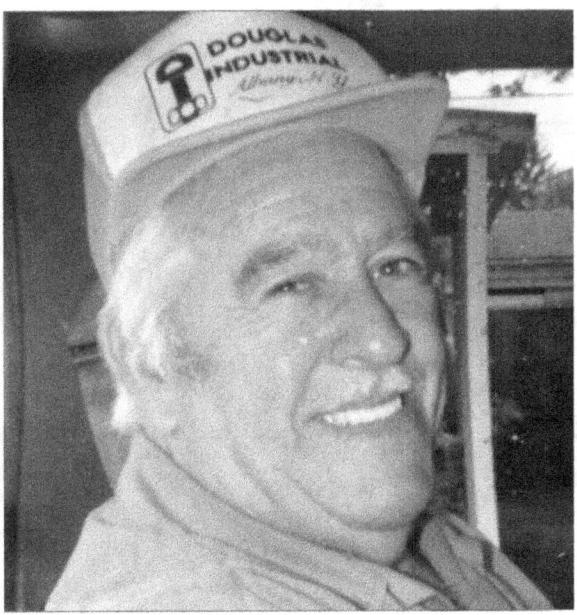
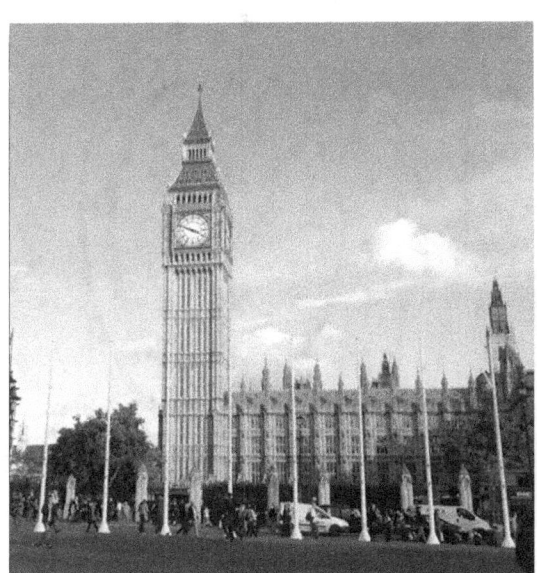
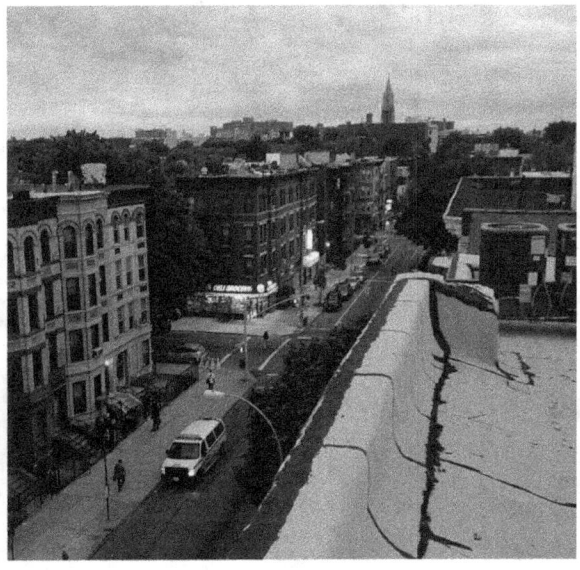

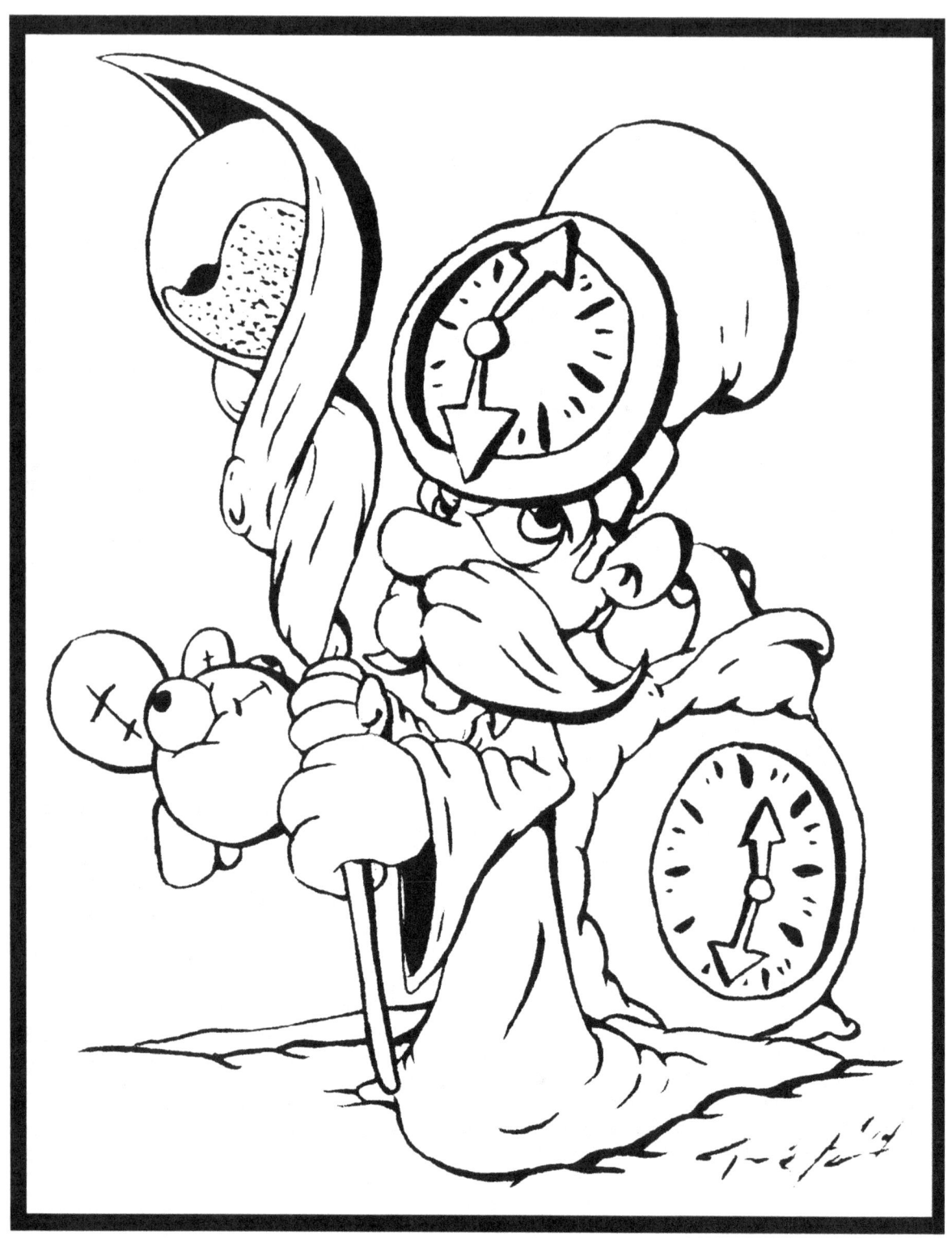

The Second Chances of Father Time

DAY 20

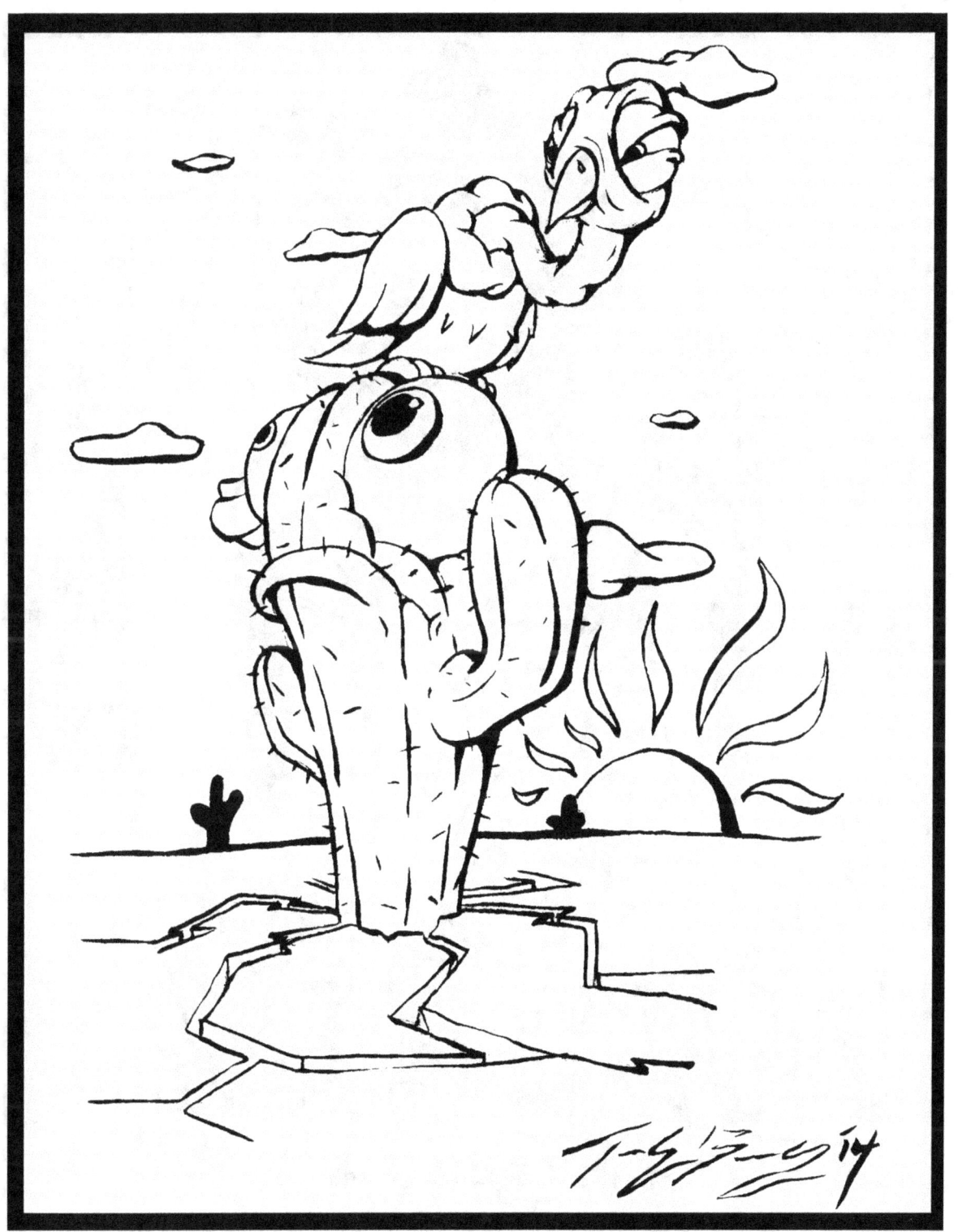

The Vultures' Reign

DAY 21

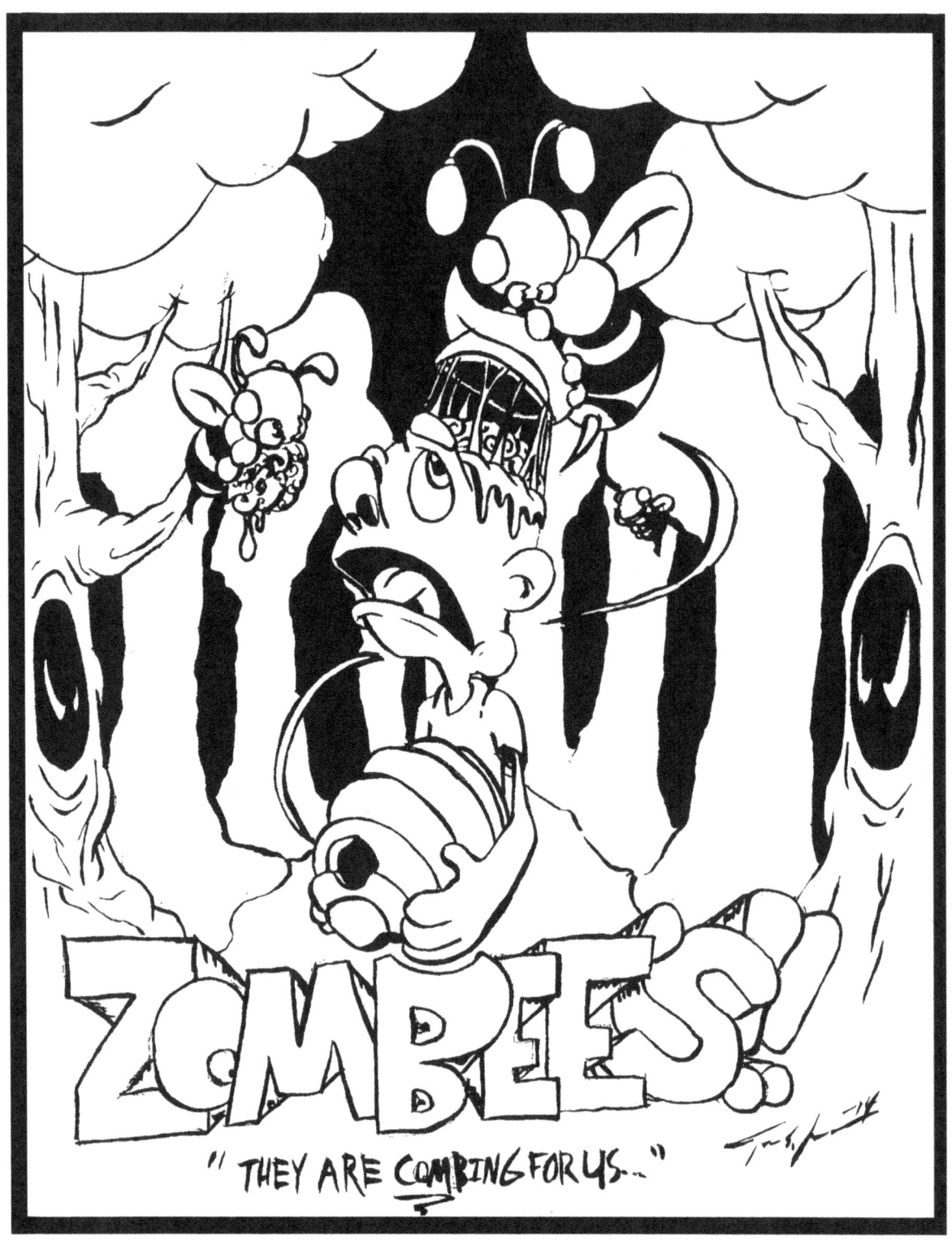

Attack of the Zombee's

DAY 22

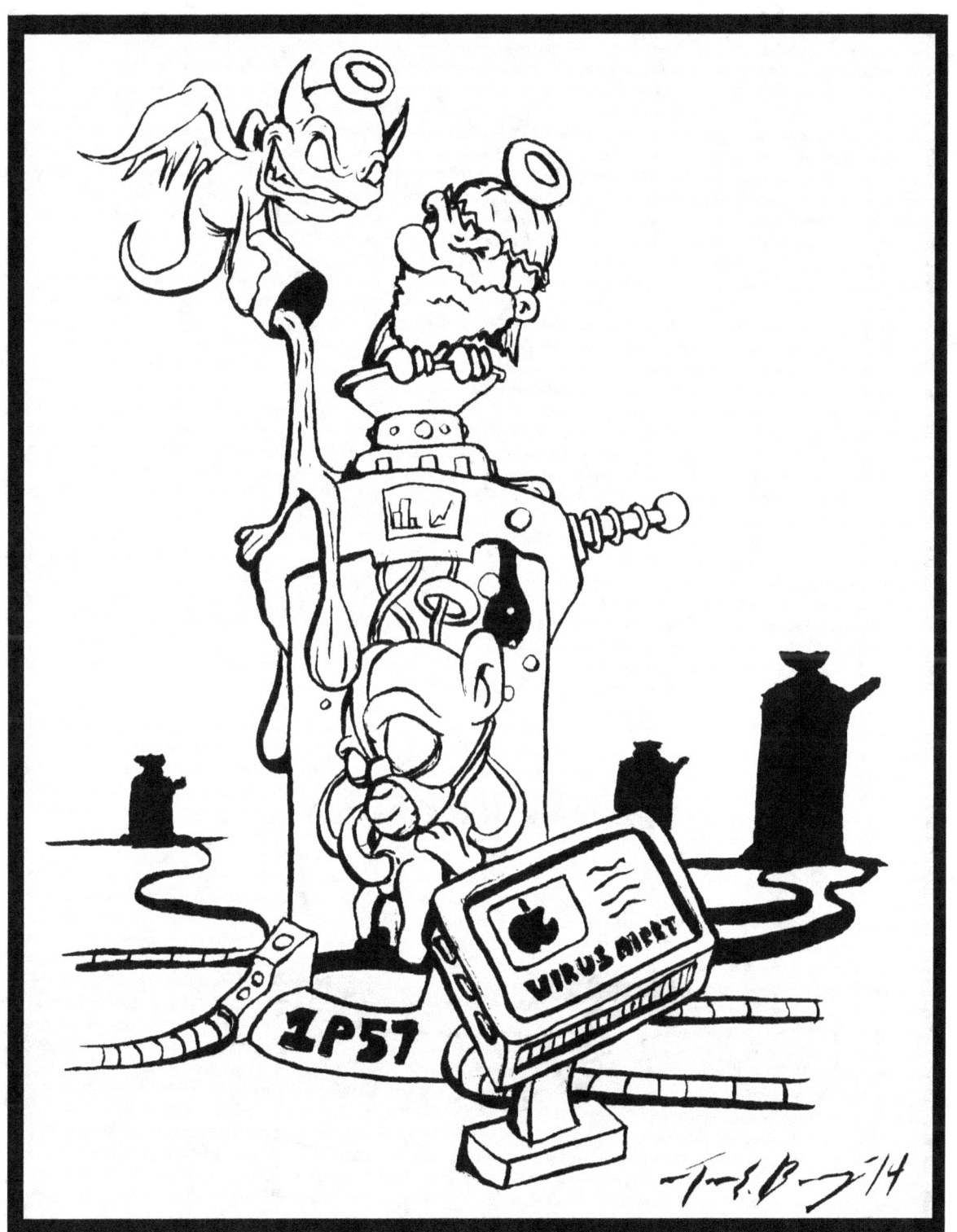

Cell Fish Intentions

DAY 23

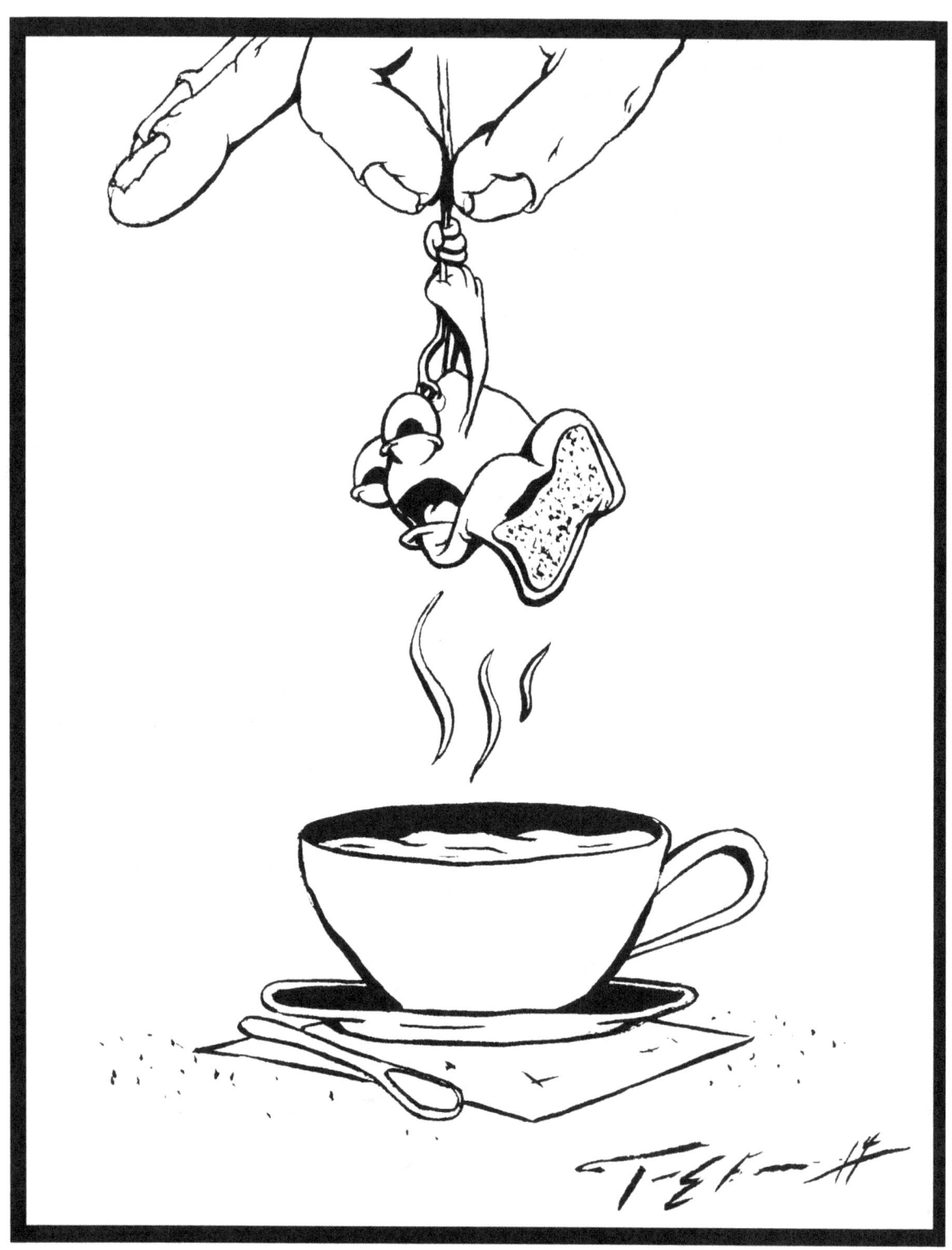

Death Is A Travis Tea

DAY 24

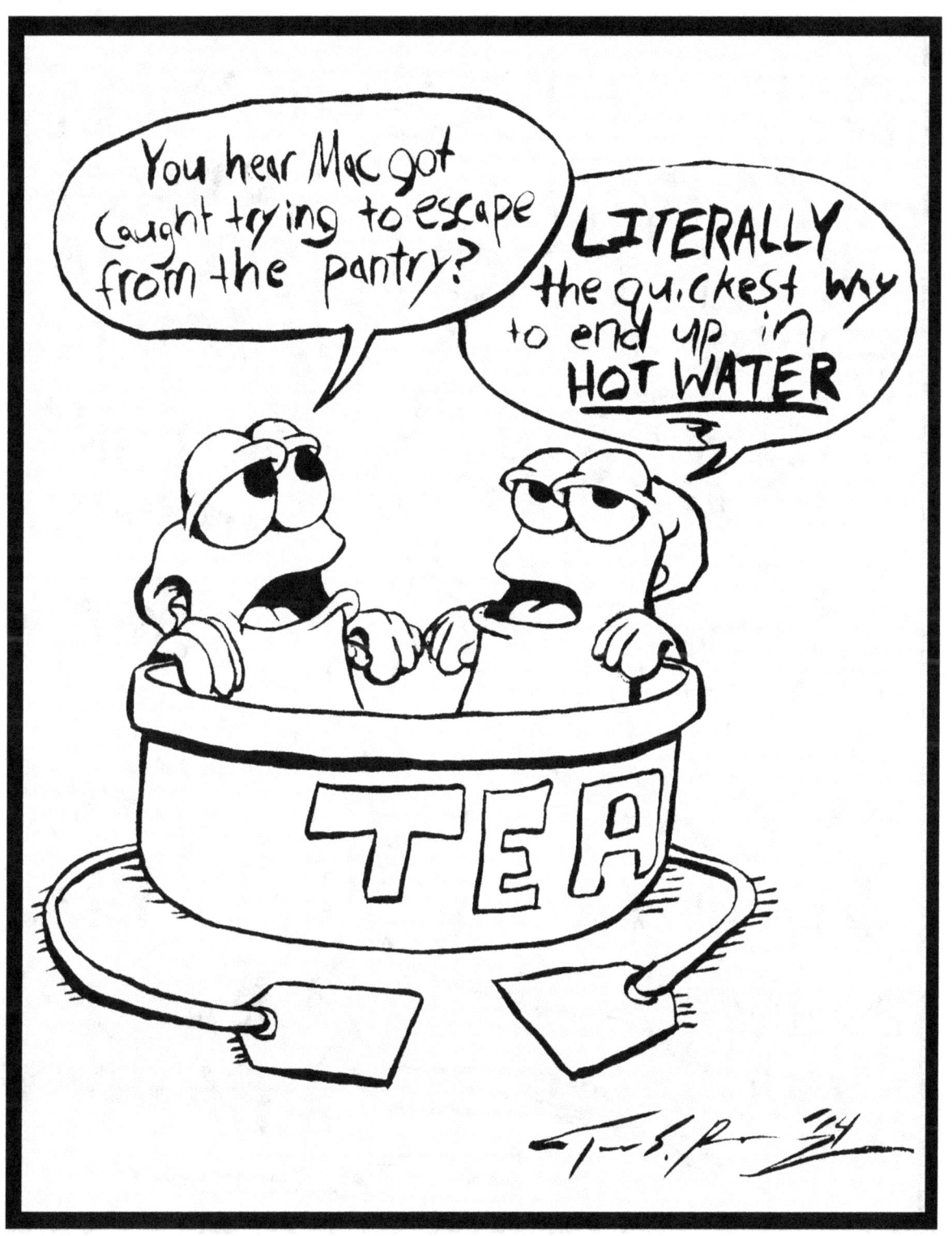

Death Is A Travis Tea (No. 2)

DAY 25

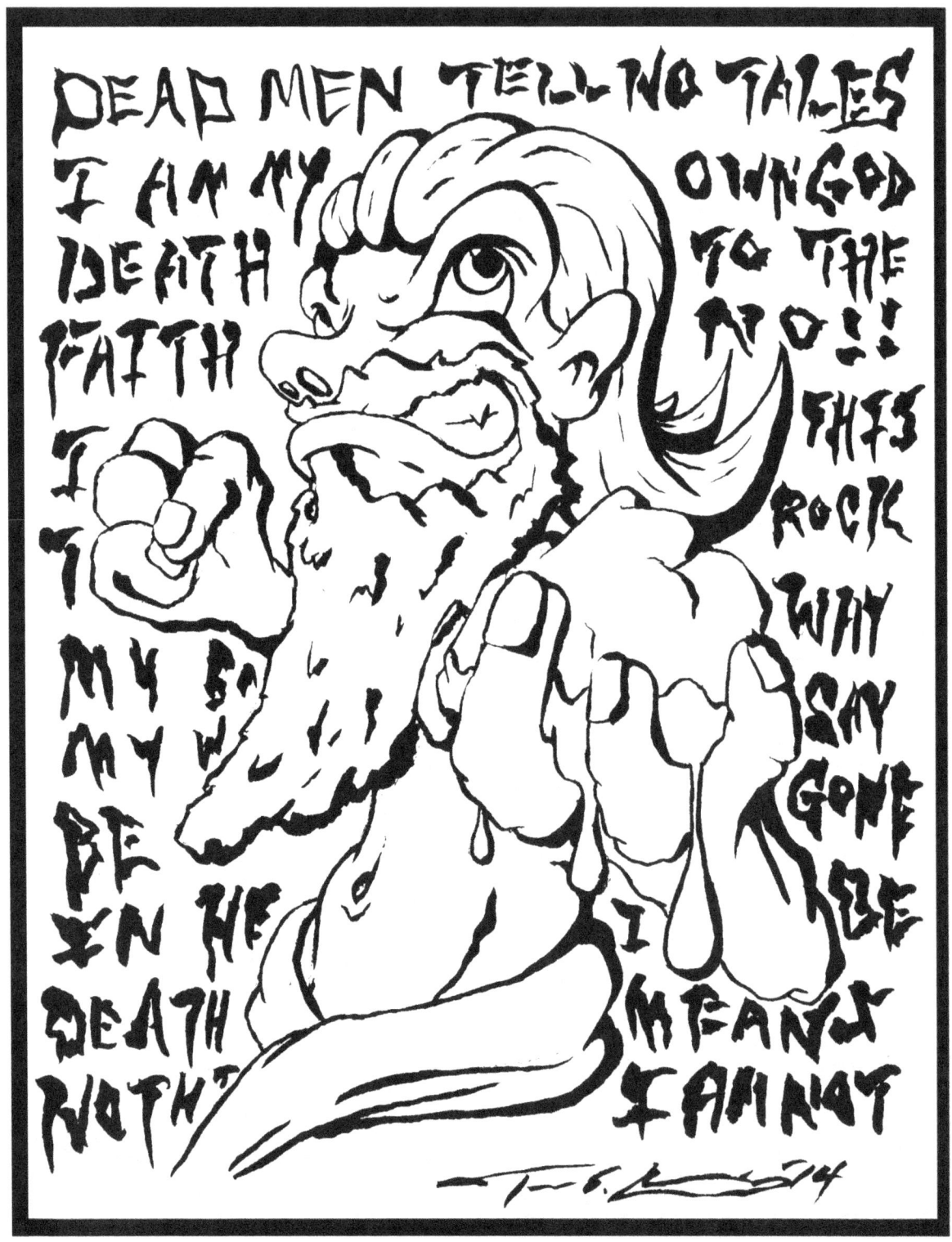

I Am (My Own God)

DAY 26

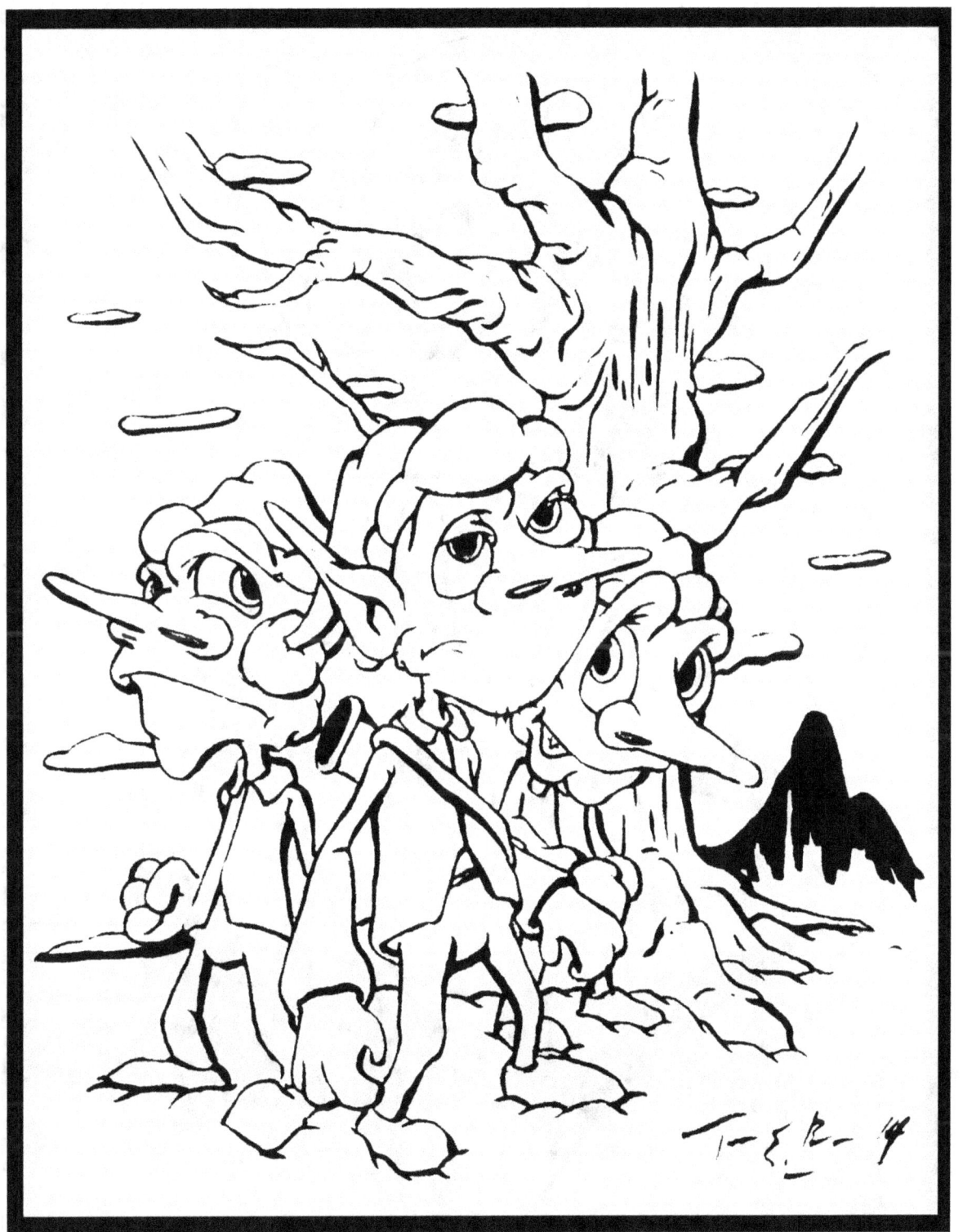

Elven Stealth Squad

DAY 27

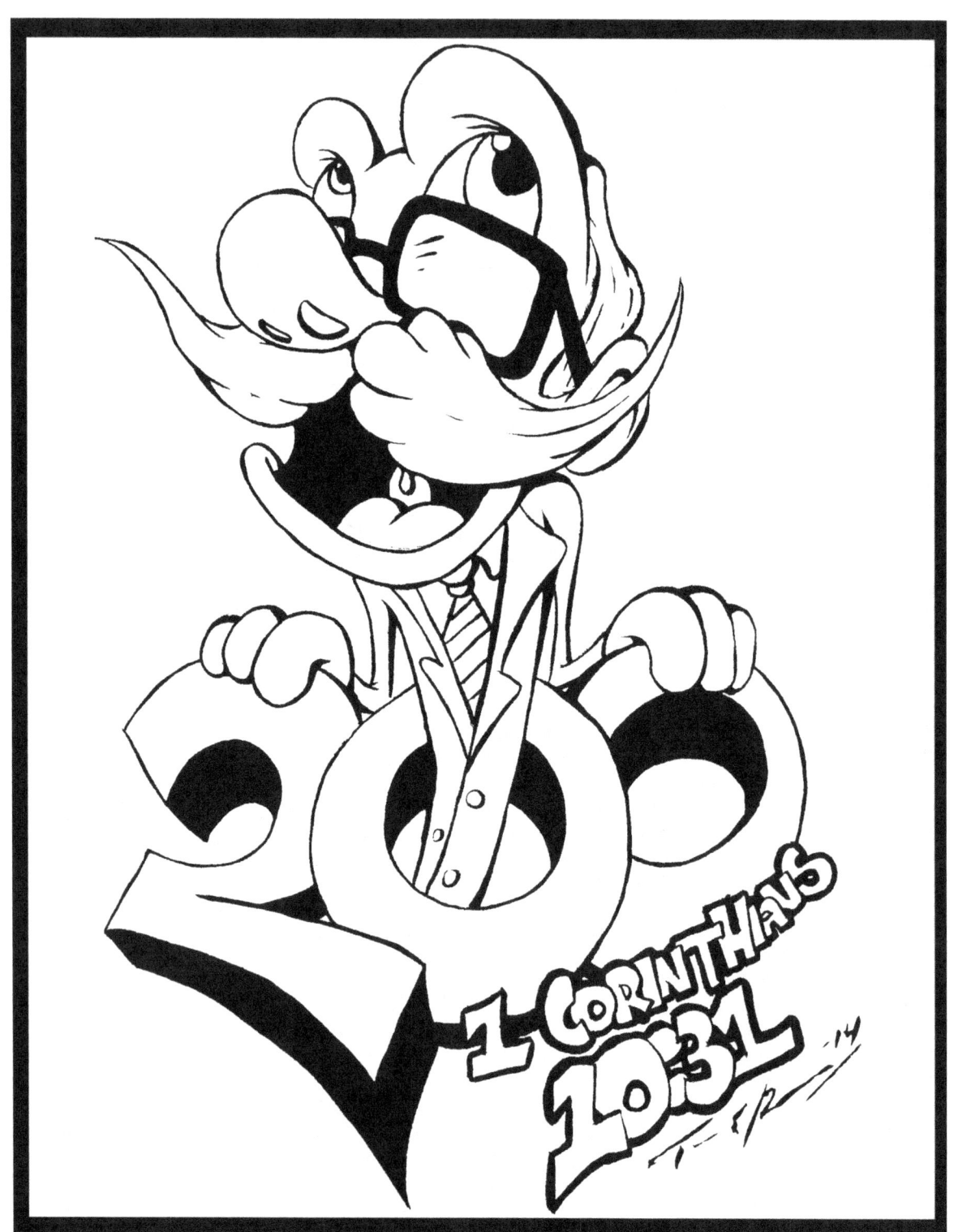

200 Followers

DAY 28

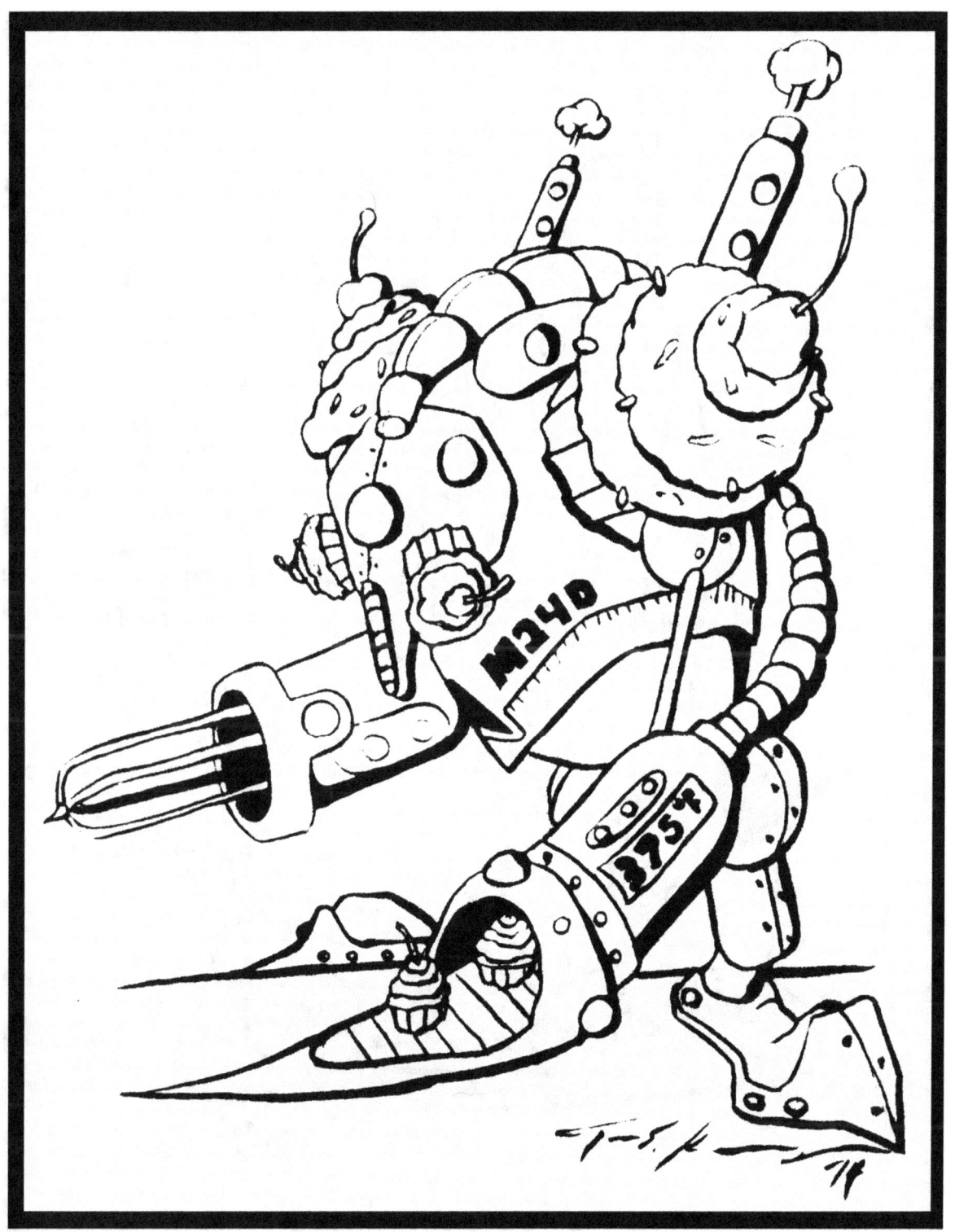

Cupcake Terror Former

DAY 29

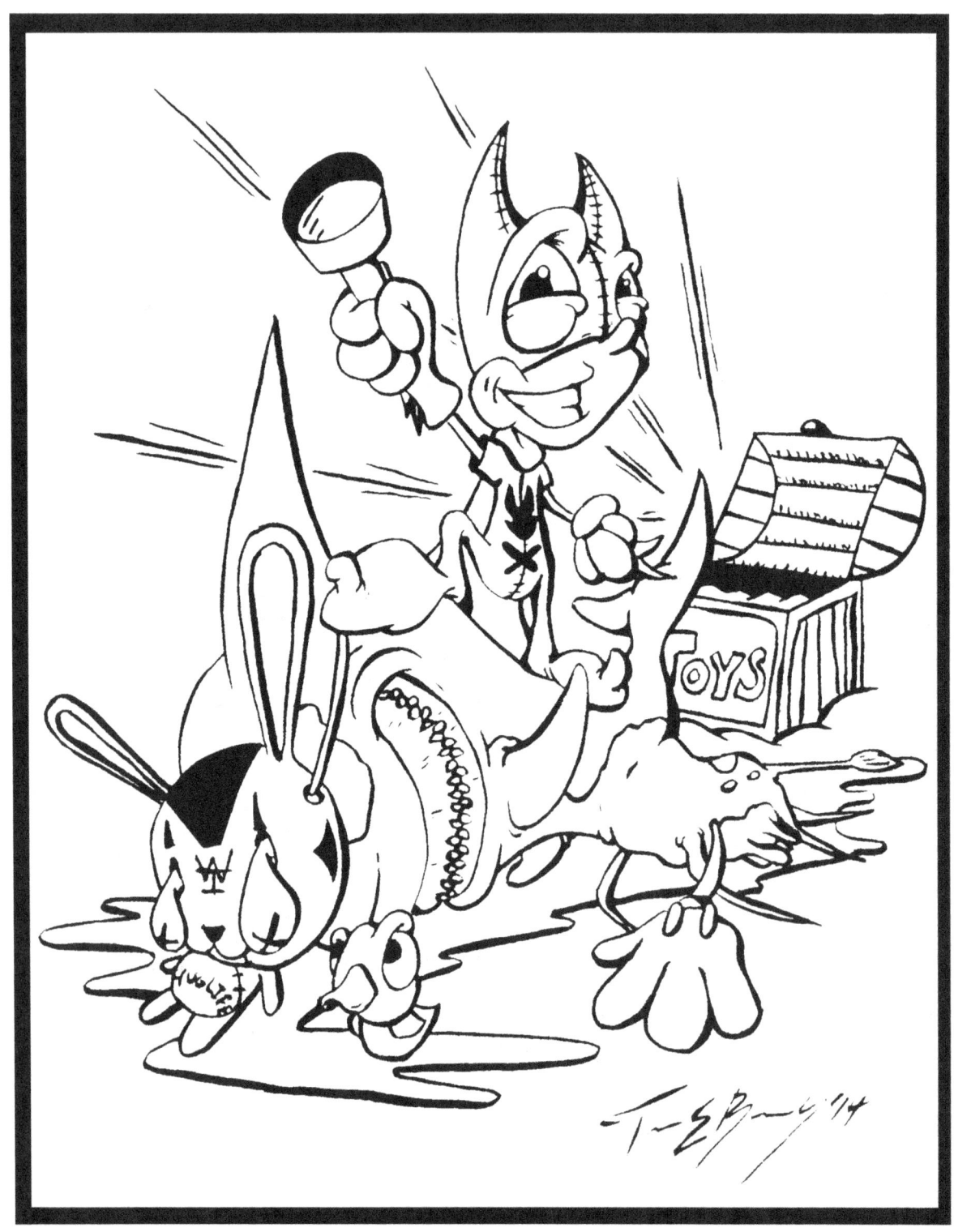

Ralf Rises On The Dark Night

DAY 30

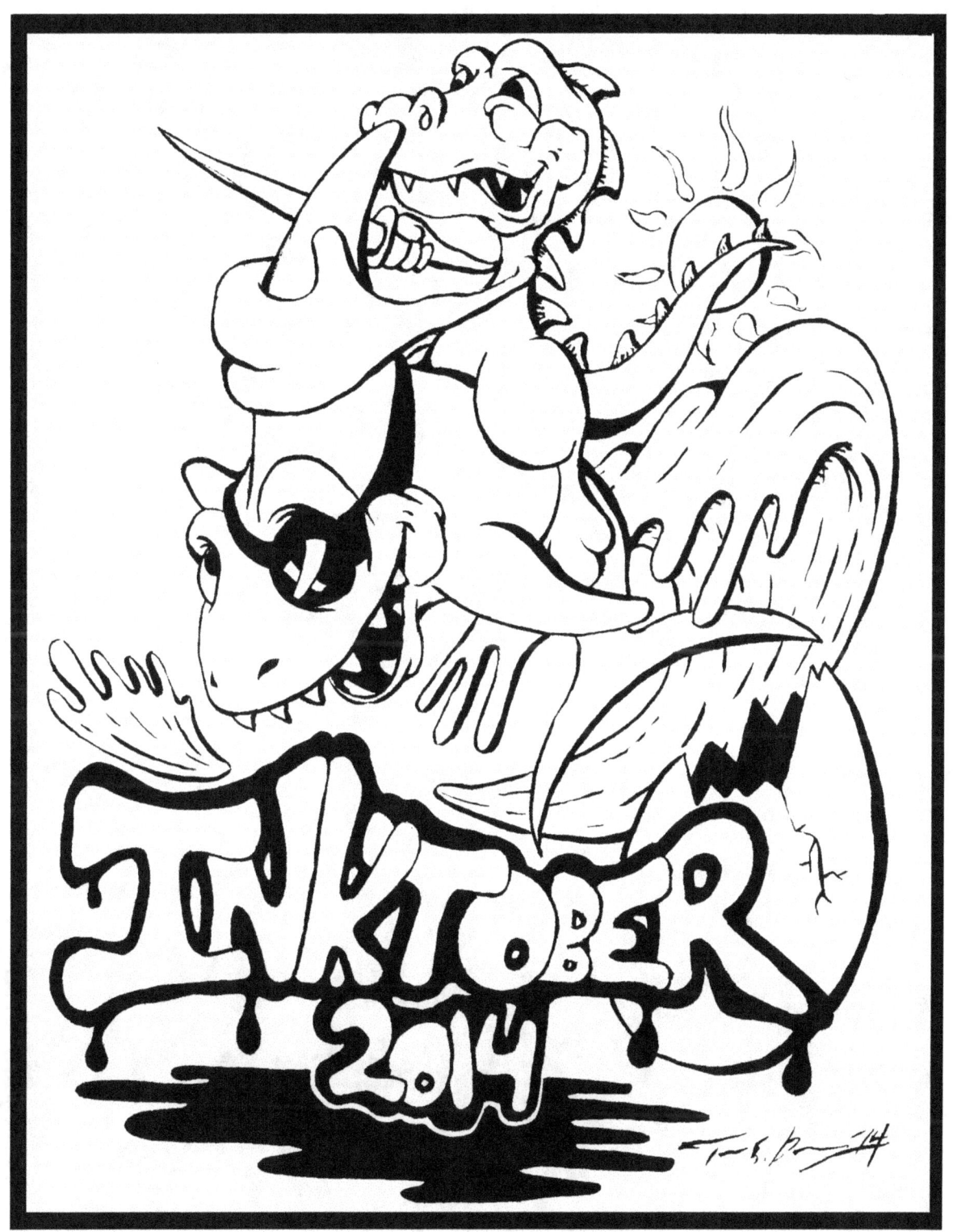

Toof & Nail (Inktober 2014)

DAY 31

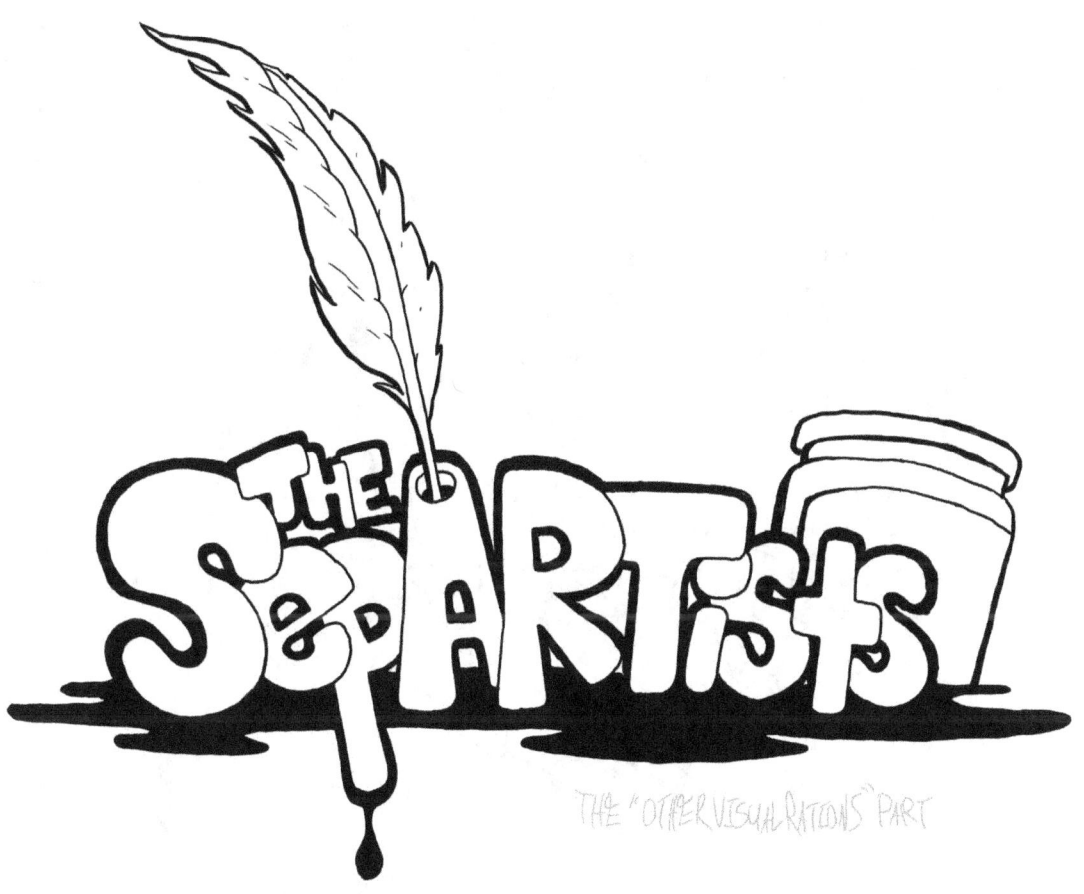

THE "OTHER VISUAL RATIONS" PART

all work dates before July 10th, 2015

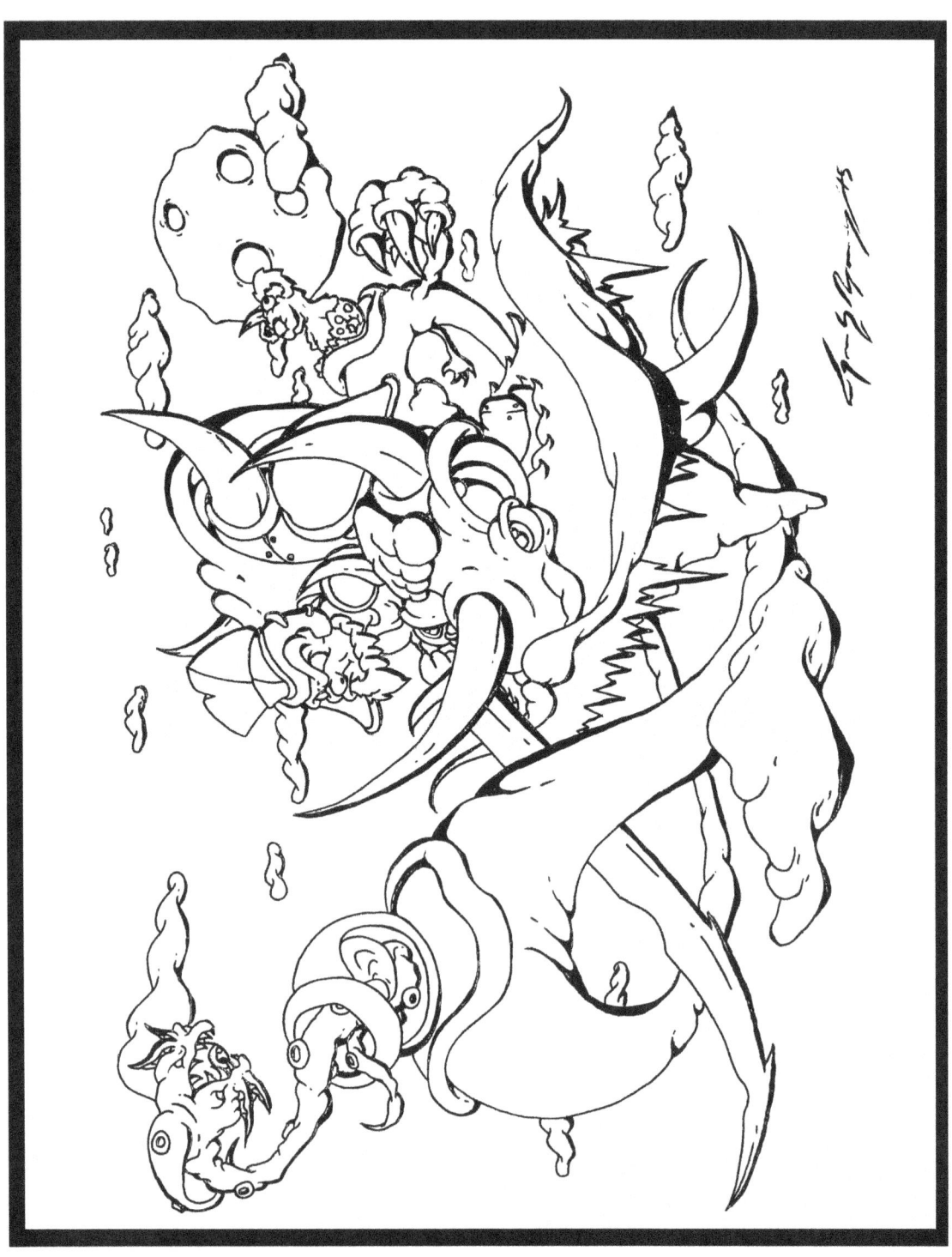

Harris & Ford

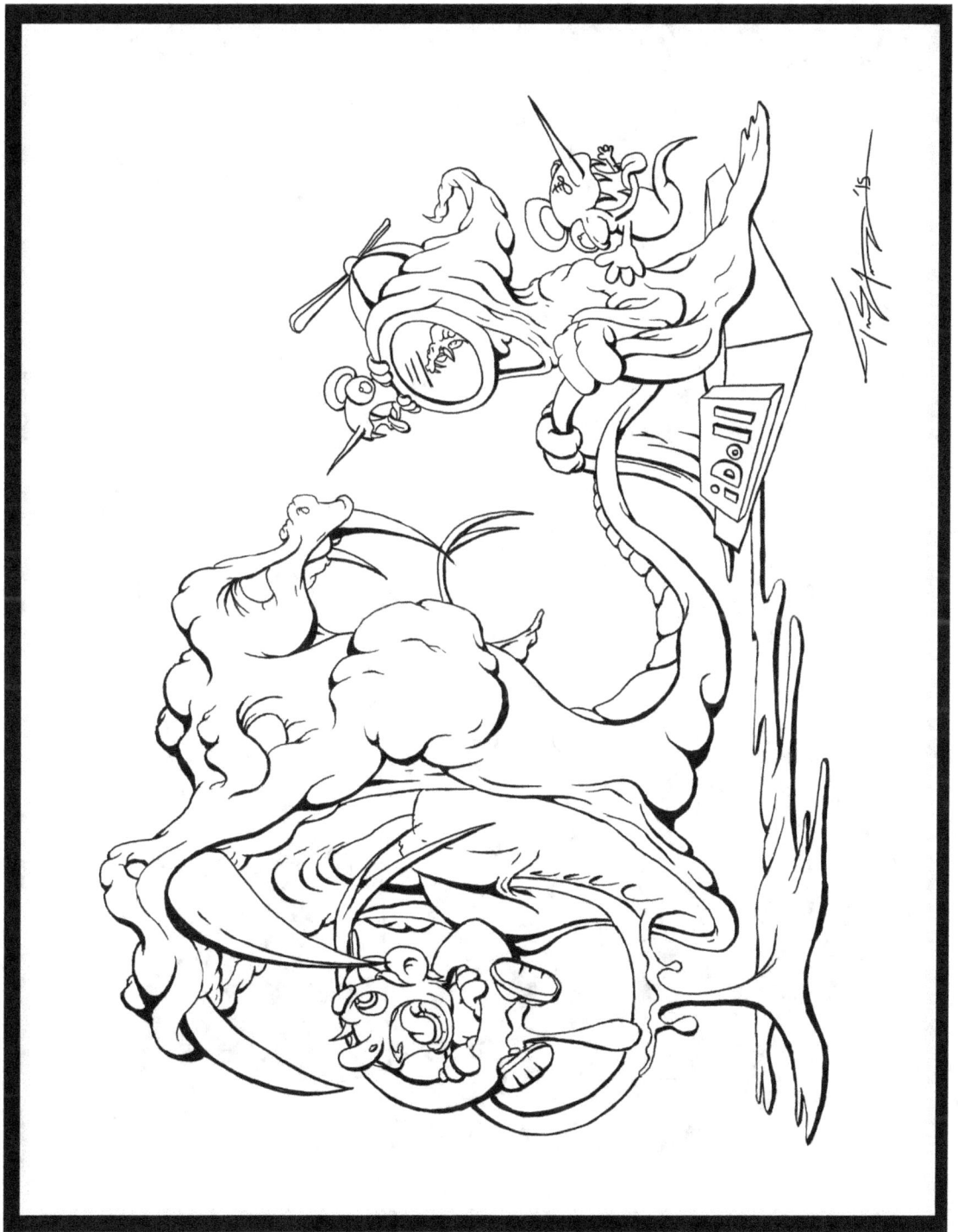

Serpentance

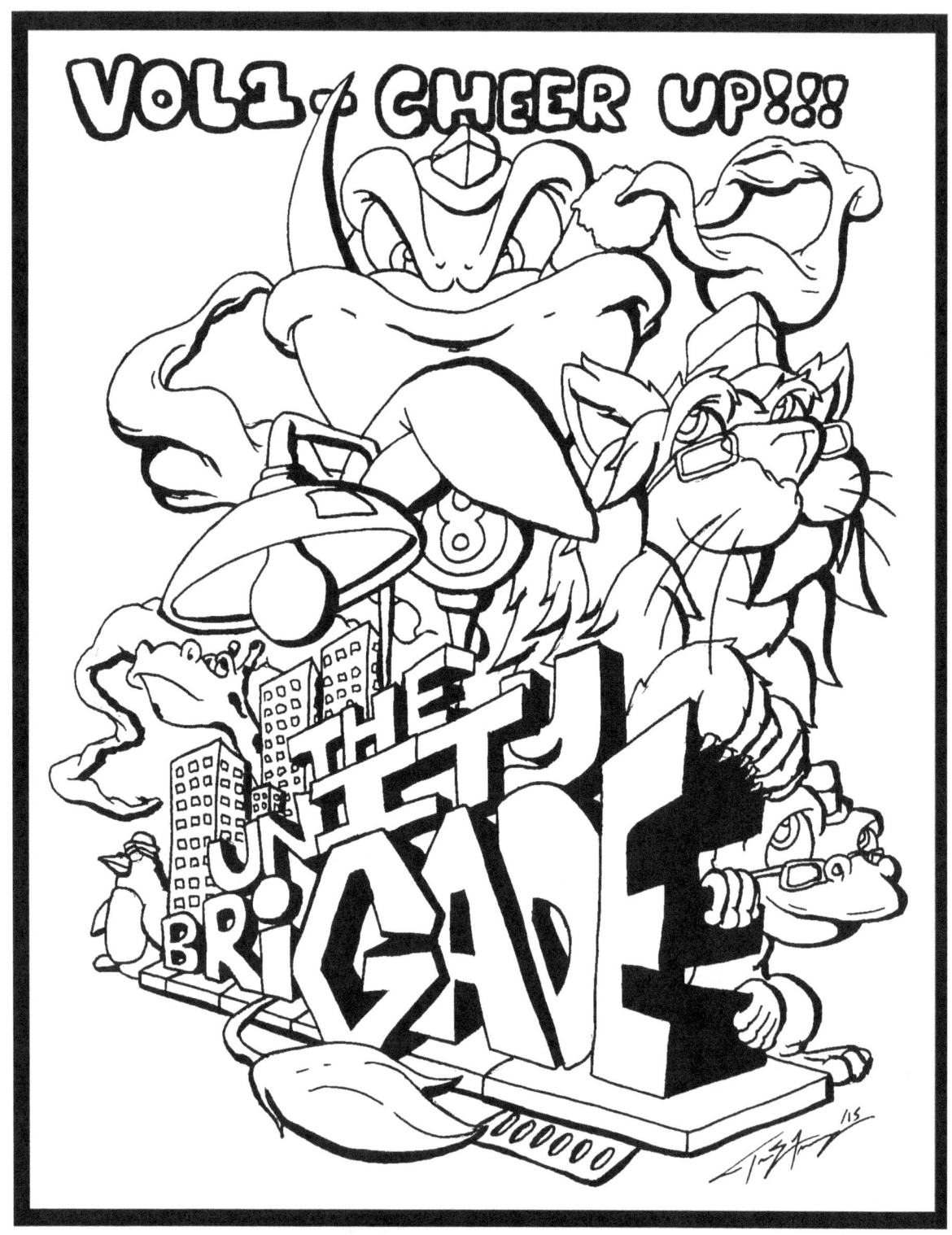

The Unity Brigade Vol.1- Cheer Up!!!

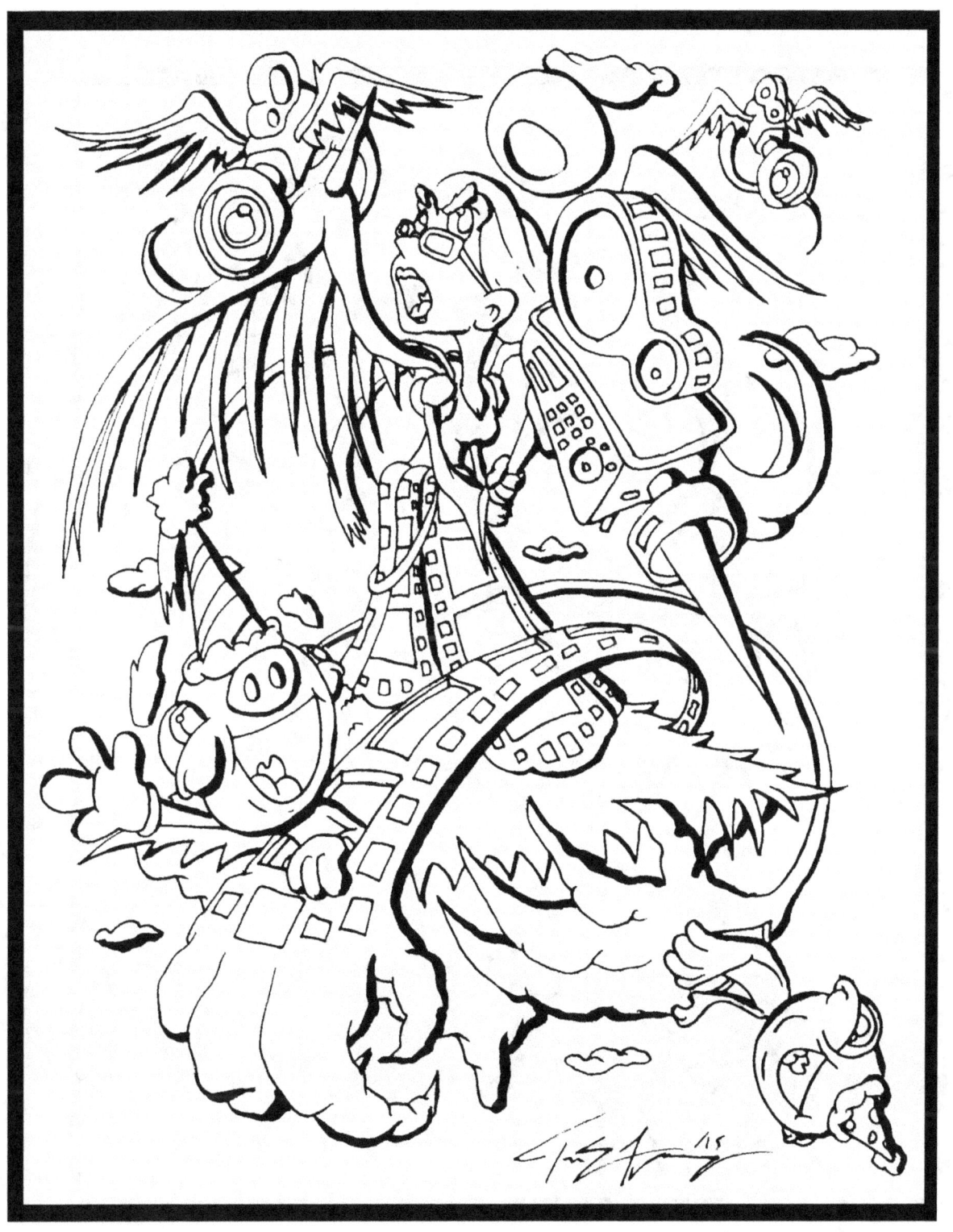

Kate the Greek Goddess of Reel Negativity

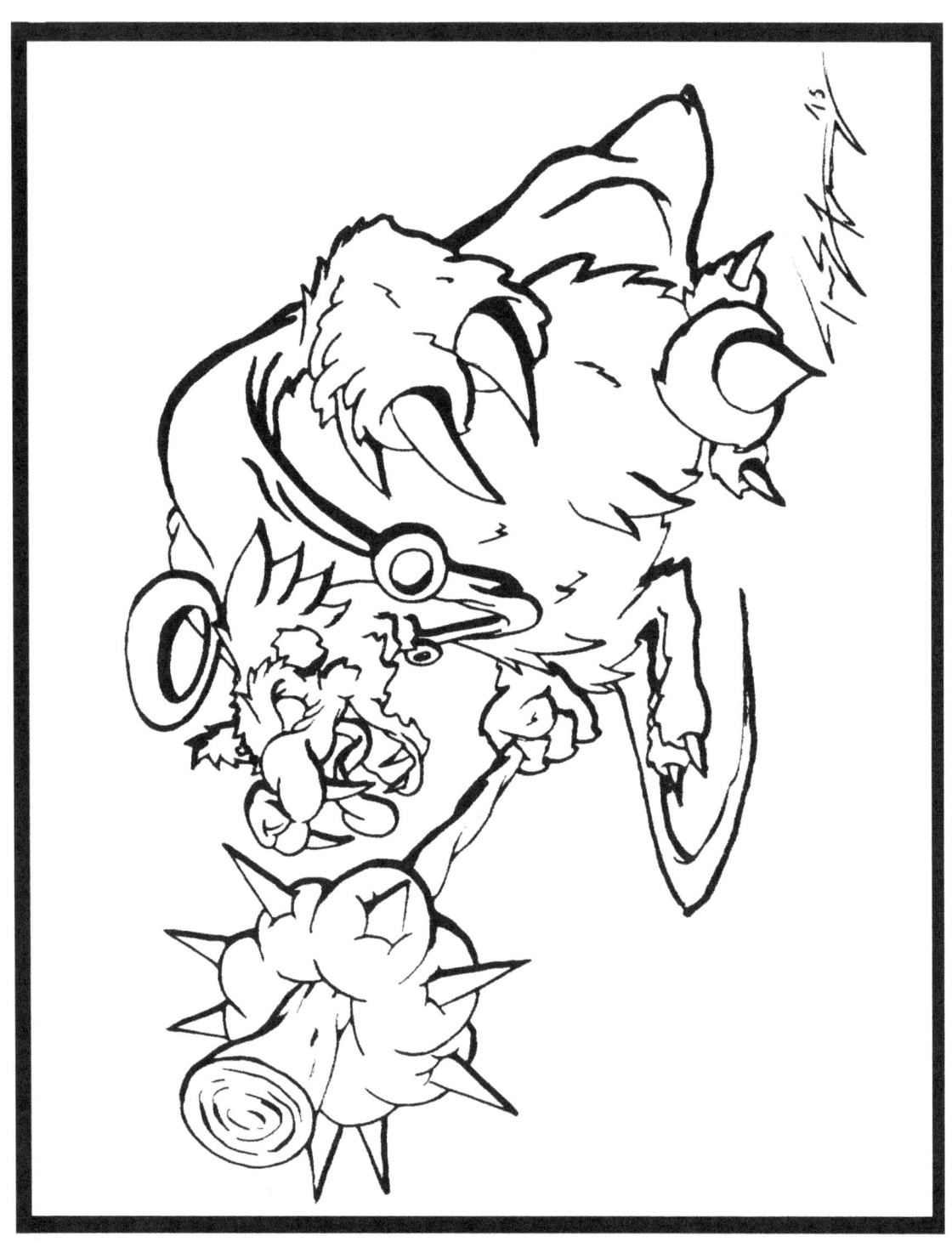

Grit the Bluff Mage

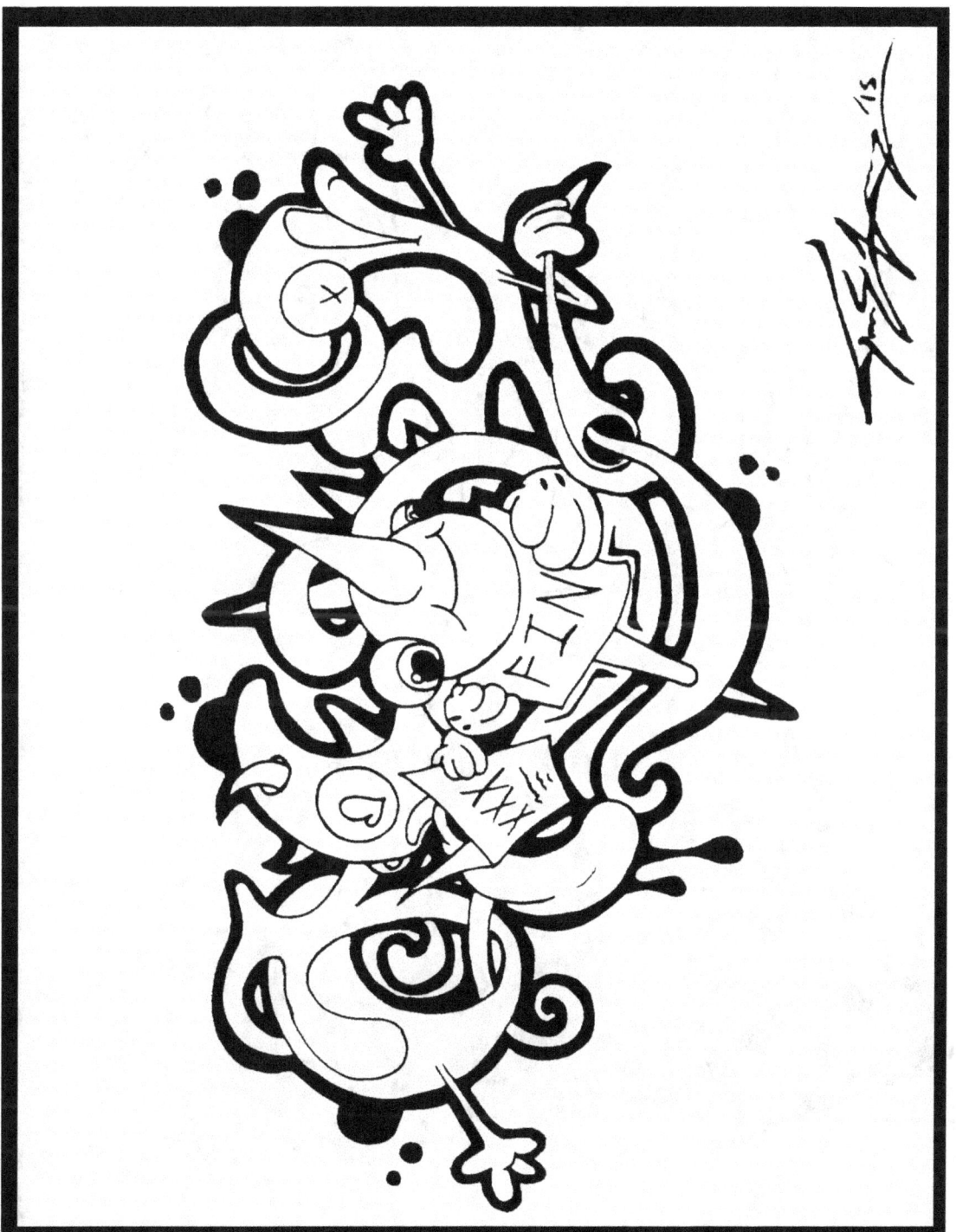

The Birth of RMNS13 (Demons)

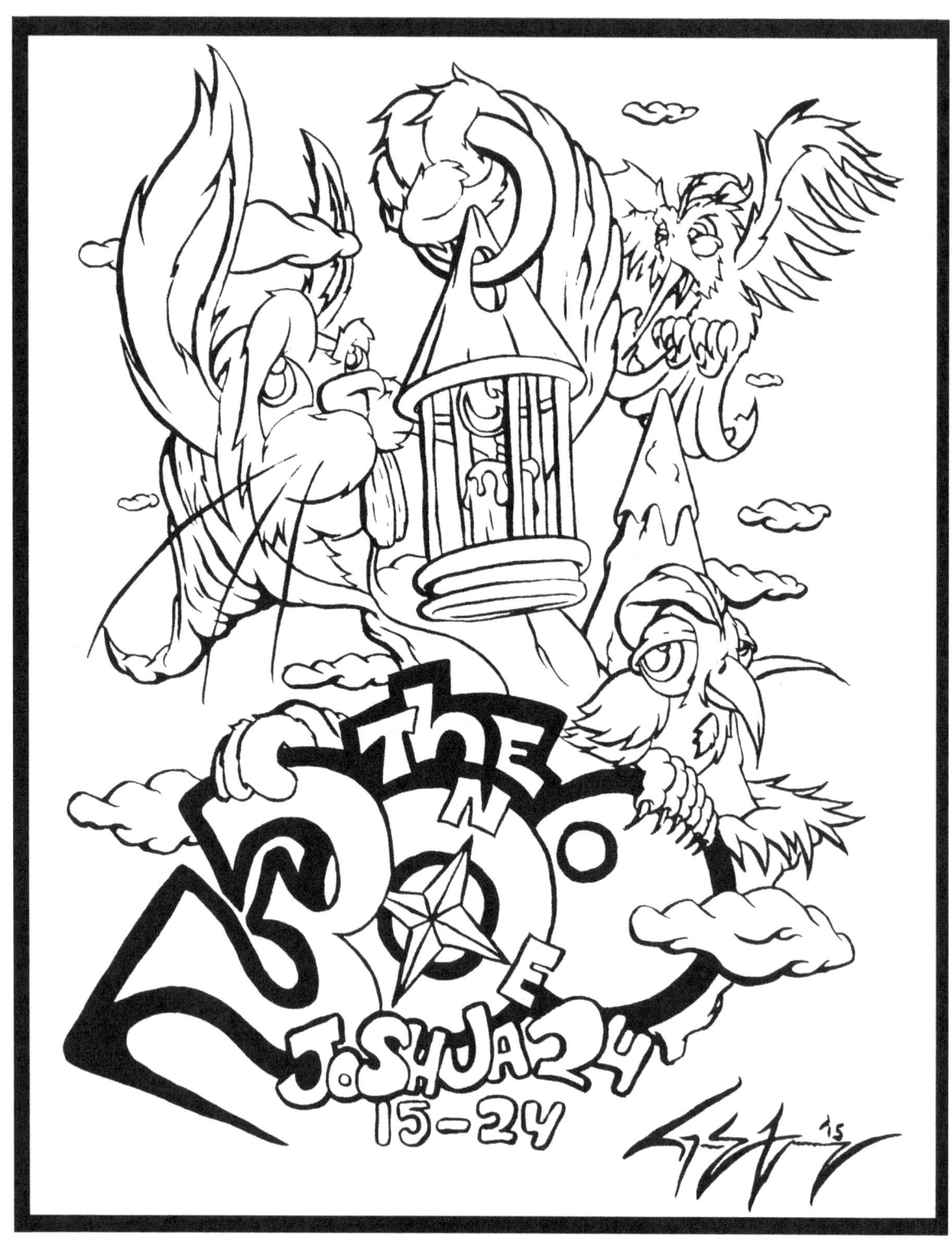

300 Followers

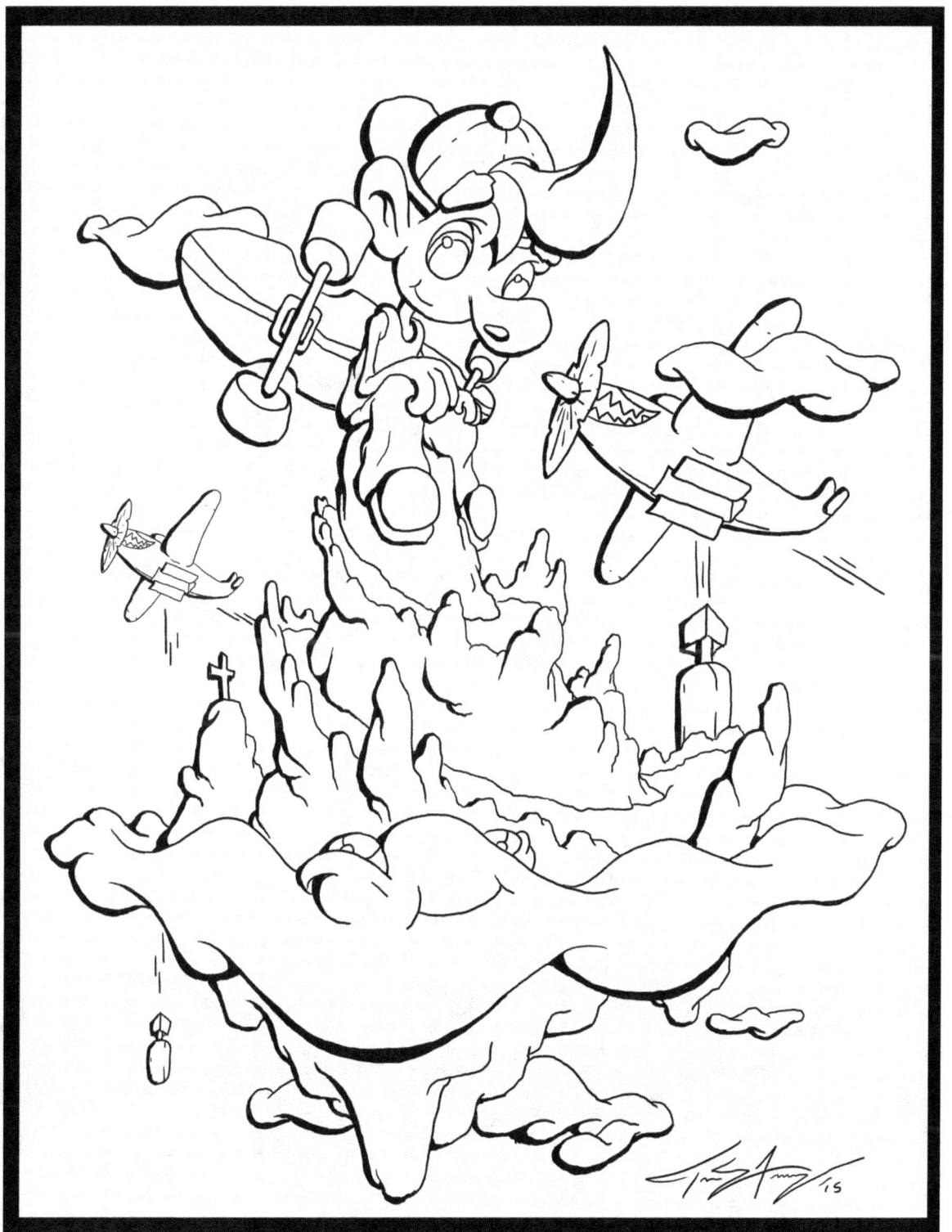

Long Boredom

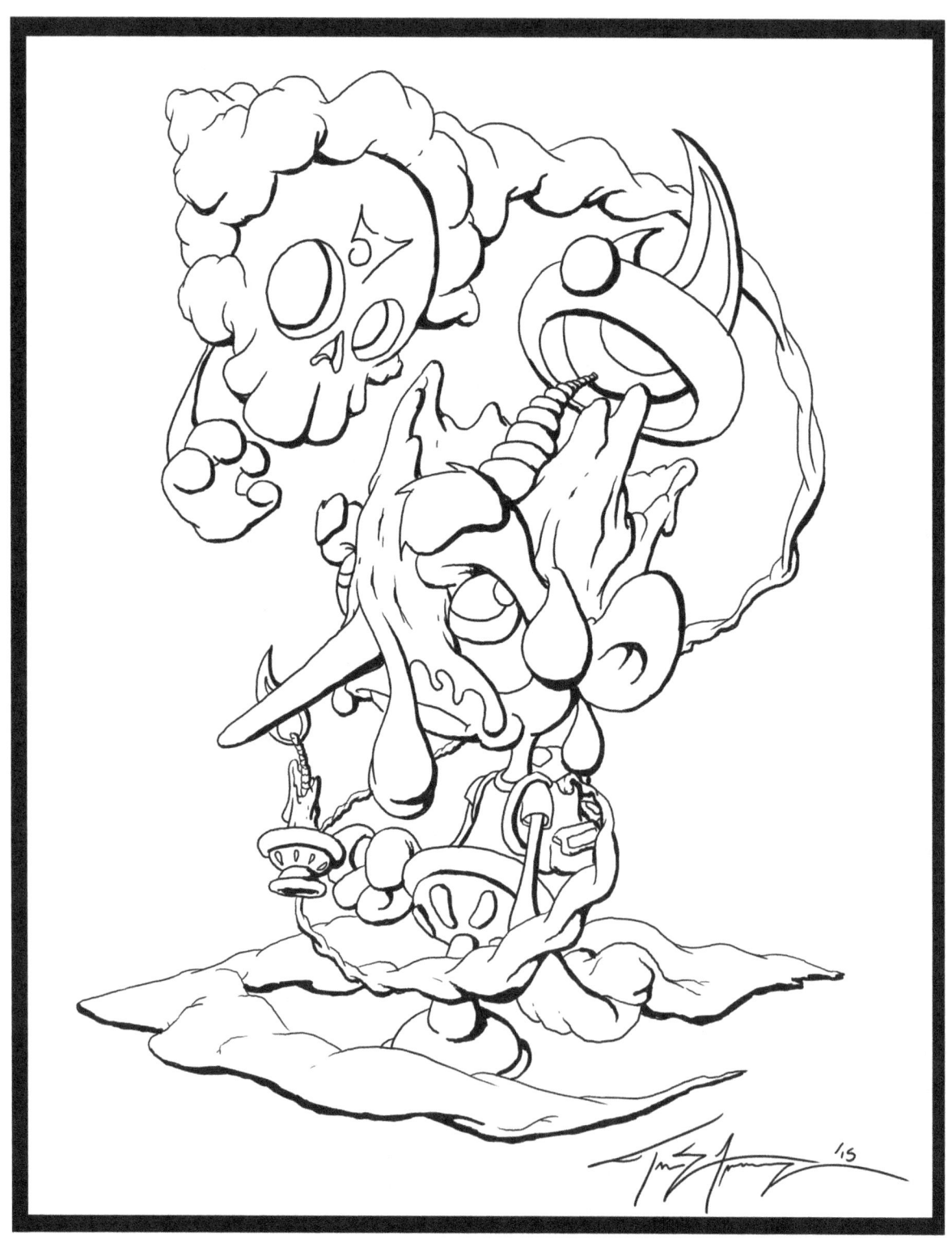

Blurryface (My Name Is...)

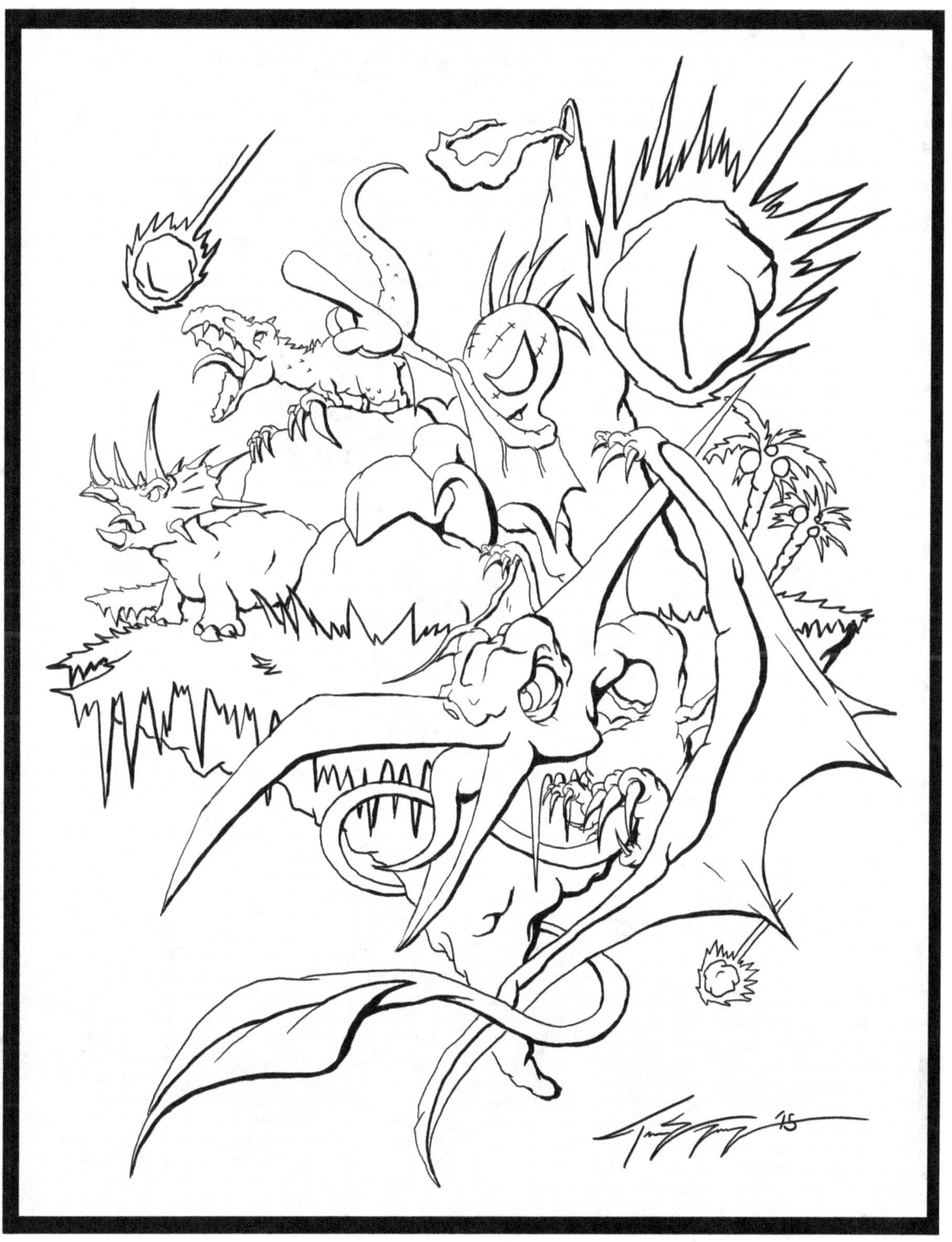

Peter Jurassic Parkers' Cometary

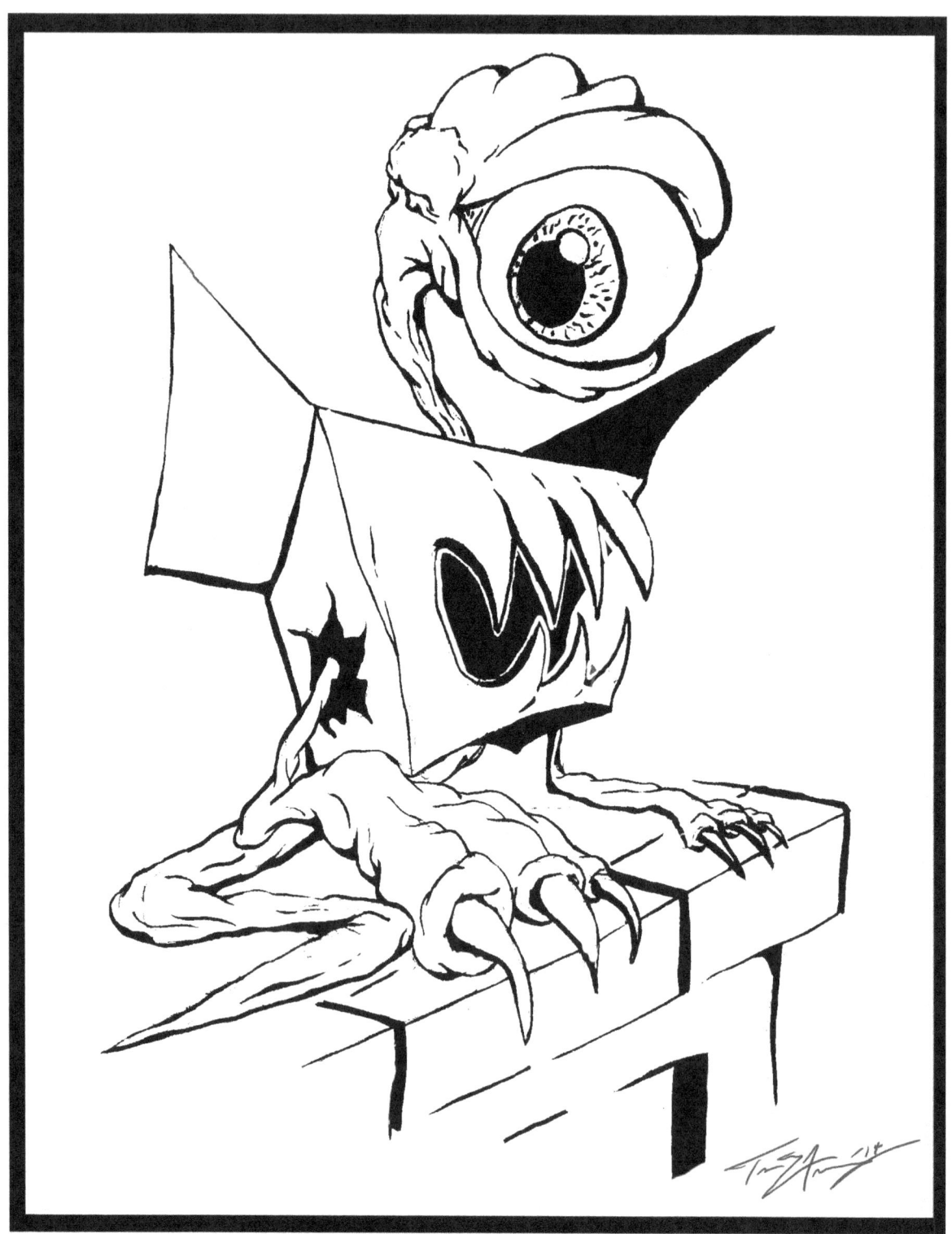

Eye Stalker

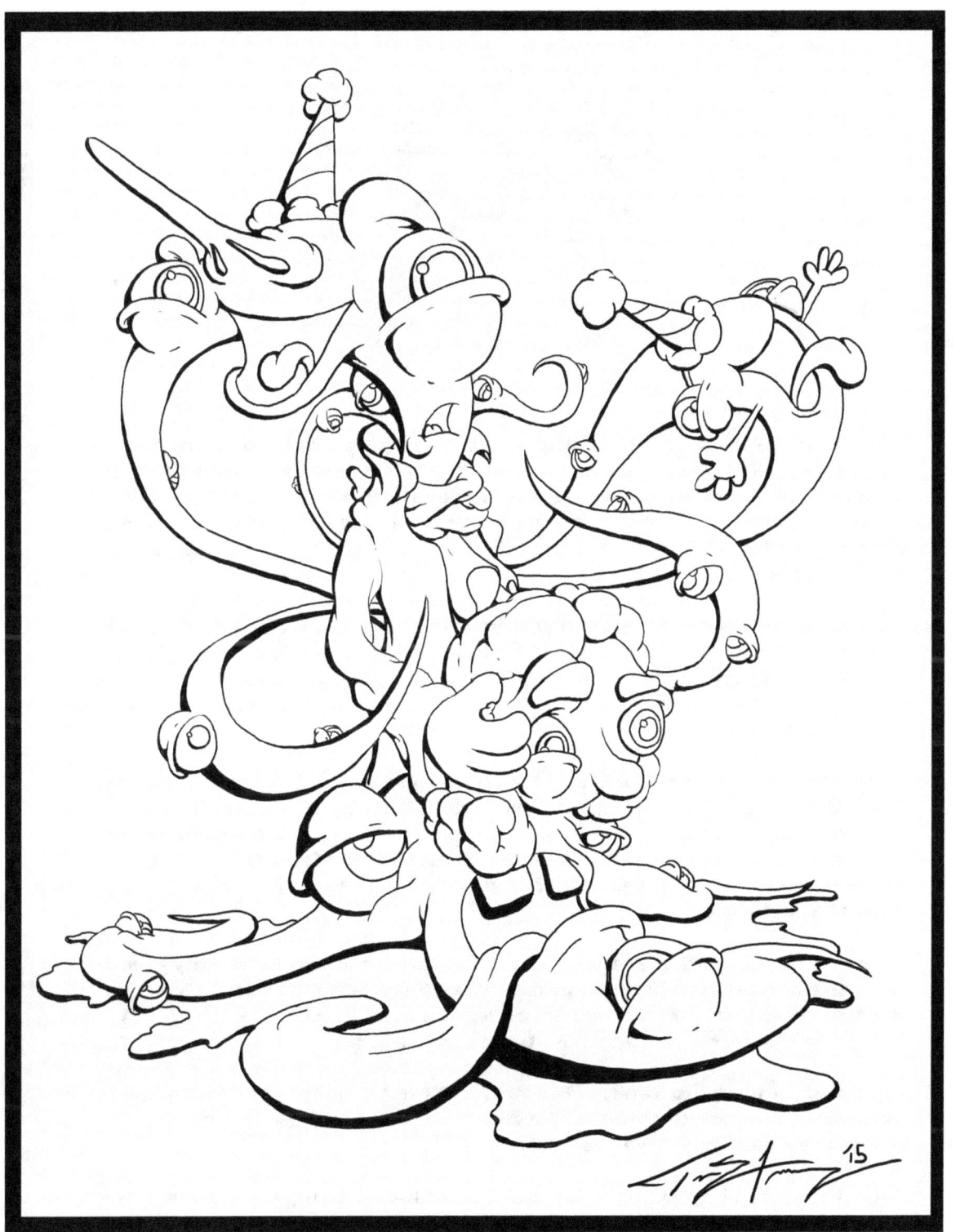

The Travis Tea Party

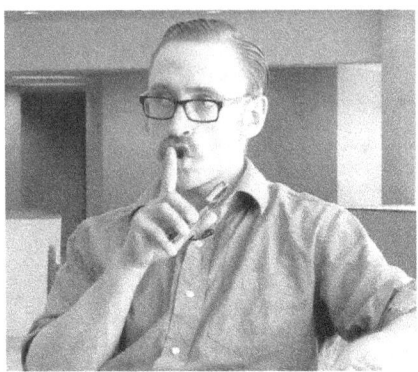

Travis "RMNS13" Bradley

What's up? My name is Travis Bradley. I tried writing this in the third person, but it was really odd so we'll just do this. You're reading this obviously to get a better understanding of who I am or maybe it's just because it's the end of the month, and you're trying to watch your data usage so you've resorted to the prehistoric art of reading text from the surface of dead trees; either way Netflix can wait.

This is probably the 4th time I'm writing this. It's that bad. The first two times I wrote this I was in a car bound for Nashville to go to my first ever Warped Tour. I'm 24. I don't have much longer. Good thing it down poured, and we left on the assurance that we could get vouchers to the St.Louis stop. Yeah. No dice. It's ok I'm over it.

So the basic stuff? I was Born, and Raised in the Capital District of New York. Now? Well now I live in Memphis, TN. Wait. What? Yeah I know. The short version is that I simply took a wrong turn on my way to work, and ended up down here. Ok. Not really. That would be ludacris, and frankly I've always been more of an Eminem fan. I actually moved down here for Seminary at Mid-America Baptist Theological.

I came to be a Christian at age 13. This was barely months before my grandfather (who this book is dedicated to) passed away. Fast forward to now I have my HS diploma, 2 years of professional art education from Pratt MWP (Utica, NY), and half of my undergrad in Christian Studies completed.

That's me. A wayward Yankee. Follower of Christ. And way too much Pokemon influence that I care to admit. I strived to cover a lot of bases of what makes me tick in the drawings you've seen in here. That's me.

I guess to close I'll tell you my lumberjack riddle... actually nevermind.
It'd probably stump you.

CONTACT INFO

ETSY: RMNS13
FACEBOOK: Travis "RMNS13" Bradley
GMAIL: RMNS13art@gmail.com
PATREON: RMNS13
INSTAGRAM: @instamistabradley
SOCIETY6: RMNS13
TUMBLR: theartofRMNS13

---

a huge shout out to
ANNA NASON

Without her patience, and aid this book may never have been completed. Go check out her work on Facebook, and Instagram:

FACEBOOK: Anna Taylor Nason Illustration
INSTAGRAM: @atn.illustration

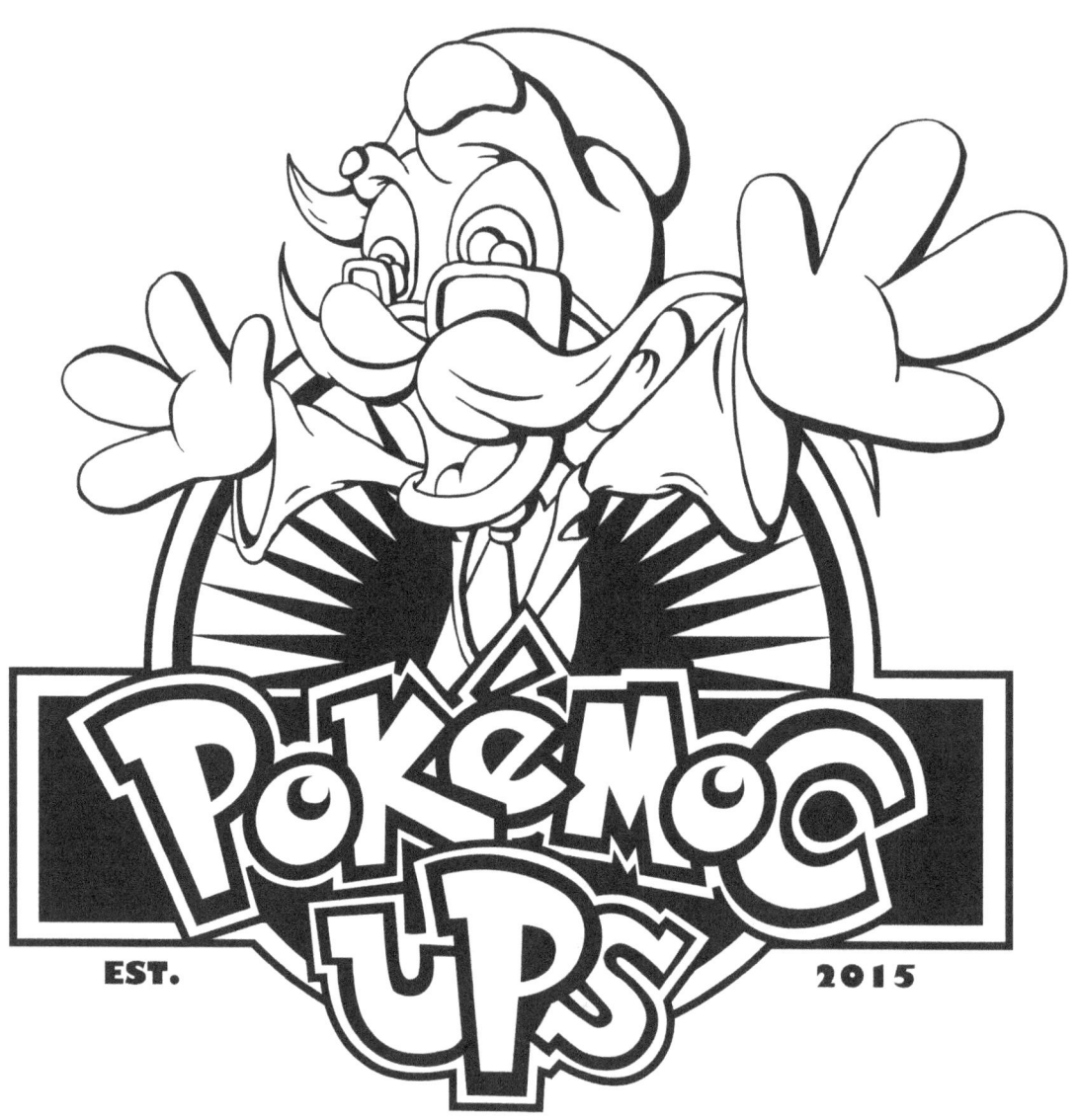

THE PATREON IS NOW OPEN

Follow the project on all previously listed Media accounts,
and please consider supporting the project along with others at
WWW.PATREON.COM/RMNS13.

TRAVIS 'RMNS13' BRADLEY'S

A D A M S

Inktober 2015 + Other Visual Rations

NEXT

www.ingramcontent.com/pod-product-compliance
Lightning Source LLC
Chambersburg PA
CBHW082302200526
45168CB00017B/2747